Perspectives on Childhood

A Resource Book for Teachers

BOB HILL, GRAHAM PIKE
AND DAVID SELBY

CASSELL

Cassell
Wellington House   PO Box 605
125 Strand   Herndon
London WC2R 0BB   VA 20172

First published 1998

British Library Cataloguing-in-Publication Data
A catalogue record for this book is available from the British Library.

ISBN 0–304–33424–3

Typeset by York House Typographic Ltd, London
Printed and bound in Great Britain by
Redwood Books, Trowbridge, Wilts

Dedication

To our children

CHILDREN
Tired of being
Harassed by your
Stupid Parents?
ACT NOW!
Move out, Get a job,
Pay your own bills,
While you still
Know everything

Children's poster

The way a society treats children reflects not only its qualities of compassion and protective caring but also its sense of justice, its commitment to the future and its urge to enhance the human condition for coming generations. This is as indisputably true of the community of nations as it is of nations individually.

Javier Pérez de Cuéllar

I have never been stopped in the street by people collecting funds for nuclear weapons. Because this has been well taken care of by governments. But I have seen many collections for children.

Peter Ustinov

'Think Positively, Travel Collectively.' A card drawn for the Norwegian Voice of the Children International Campaign

PERSPECTIVES ON CHILDHOOD

Also available from Cassell:
J. McGuiness: *Counselling in Schools*
S. Roffey, T. Tarrant and K. Majors: *Young Friends*

Contents

How to use this book

The matrix opposite is intended as a handy guide to which activities most directly address the key concepts and ideas in sections 1 and 2 of the Introduction.

Resource requirements as given with each activity are based on a class size of 30 students unless otherwise indicated. The timings are approximate and refer only to the activity as described under **Procedure**. Teachers should bear in mind that discussion and debriefing are essential aspects of the learning process and sufficient time should be allowed for these to take place. Teachers should note that the symbol P means that the material on that page can be photocopied for use within the institution purchasing the book. The activities, save where separately acknowledged, were developed by the authors.

KEY CONCEPTS AND IDEAS

Campaigning/action for children's rights	Student rights	Learning entitlement	Child exploitation	Child labour	Child abuse/harassment	Discrimination	Rights denials/violations	Responsibilities	Participation rights	Protection rights	Development rights	Children's rights	Childrearing	Legal age/rights	Rites of passage	Gender	Cultural perspectives	Socialization	Adulthood	Childhood	Identity	Activities
																	●				●	Activity 1
																	●	●			●	Activity 2
																	●				●	Activity 3
																	●	●		●	●	Activity 4
																●	●	●			●	Activity 5
															●	●	●			●	●	Activity 6
														●	●	●	●		●	●	●	Activity 7
													●	●		●	●	●	●	●	●	Activity 8
													●			●	●	●				Activity 9
																●	●	●		●		Activity 10
																●	●				●	Activity 11
●									●	●	●	●				●			●	●		Activity 12
		●	●	●	●	●	●		●	●	●	●				●	●					Activity 13
●								●		●	●	●										Activity 14
●					●	●	●		●	●	●	●										Activity 15
			●		●	●	●			●	●			●		●				●		Activity 16
			●	●	●		●			●	●	●		●		●	●			●		Activity 17
			●	●			●			●	●	●		●						●		Activity 18
●	●	●					●	●	●							●	●					Activity 19
●	●					●	●		●	●	●	●			●	●						Activity 20
●									●													Activity 21

Acknowledgements

This publication has arisen out of a Perspective Consciousness Project undertaken at the Centre for Global Education at the University of York between 1985 and 1991 and funded by Christian Aid, the European Community, Gulbenkian Foundation, Joseph Rowntree Charitable Trust, Oxfam, the School Curriculum Development Committee, UNICEF-UK and the World Wide Fund for Nature. The work on childhood within the Project was specifically commissioned by UNICEF-UK.

The authors would like to thank the many teachers who participated in the Project. Particular thanks are also due to those who worked on the Project in their capacity as Research or Centre Fellows – David Dunetz, Yvonne Kupsch, Sandy Parker, and as Visiting Fellows – Margaret Calder, David Elton, Doug Hewitt.

Special thanks are owed to Lizz Ringer, who typed the manuscript, and to Gail Slavin, Centre Secretary, who supported us in the task of manuscript preparation in so many ways. We are grateful to Pam Ko, Secretary of the International Institute for Global Education at the University of Toronto, for subsequently updating and amending the manuscript and to Janet Munro of the Institute for also contributing to the updating process.

The following also have our thanks for their help: Jenny Coates, Training Administrator, National Society for the Prevention of Cruelty to Children; Kristin Eskeland, Northern Secretariat, Voice of the Children International Campaign; Heather Jarvis, Education Officer, UNICEF-UK; Dan Jones, Amnesty International British Section; Barbara Vellacott, Head of Education Section, Christian Aid; the embassies of Argentina, Brazil, Costa Rica, Italy, Sweden and Turkey; the Japan Information and Cultural Centre, London; the High Commissions of Australia, Canada, India and Kenya.

The publishers would like to thank the following for permission to reproduce copyright material:
Blackwell Publishers: extracts from A. Vittachi, *Stolen Childhood* (pp. 44 and 47);
Cover Stories: article from *New Statesman and Society*, 10 February 1984 (p. 69); and for extracts from *New Internationalist* **76** (pp. 35–7 and 68);
Earthscan Publications Ltd: extracts from Peter Lee-Wright, *Child Slaves* (pp. 43, 46, 48 and 67);
The Independent: article by John Pilger (pp. 53–5);
Institute of Pacific Studies, The University of the South Pacific: extracts from *Pacific Profiles*, ed. R.A.C. Stewart (pp. 21 and 26);
Shyrose Jaffer: article (pp. 56–8), originally published in *Toronto Star*, 3 November 1991;
Nigel Parbury: extract from *Survival: A History of Aboriginal Life in New South Wales* (p. 2);
Royal Anthropological Institute of Great Britain and Ireland: extracts from articles in *Anthropology Today* **1** (5) by V. Goddard (p. 67) and **4** (2) by Wendy Schottman (pp. 3–4);
UNICEF UK: article by Damien Personnaz from their *Annual Review 1995/1996* (p. 70);
Voice of the Children International Campaign, Norway: Children's Appeal to World Leaders, Rio de Janeiro, June 1992 (pp. 10–11).

Every effort has been made to trace and acknowledge the copyright owners of material reproduced in this book; if any unacknowledged copyright owners contact the publishers, the appropriate acknowledgement will appear in any future editions.

Introduction

This book explores perspectives on childhood, the socialization of children and children's rights and seeks to point up what is particular and what is universal about how we view children and their needs.

1. Childhood: some cultural perspectives

(Note: The key concepts and ideas printed in italics in this and section 2 form the basis of the matrix on p. ix).

In every society children grow up experiencing similar physical changes, such as losing milk teeth, gaining height and weight, menstruating or voice breaking. The impact of these developments on children, however, differs from one culture to another, according to the meaning which any society invests in the concept of *childhood* and the process of childrearing.

The experience of childhood is influenced by a combination of personal attributes – including *gender*, ethnicity, physical appearance, abilities/disabilities – and social determinants, such as culture, religion and class. As children grow up their view of themselves and of the world is shaped, too, by the 'agents' of socialization: parents and family, peer groups, schools and mass media. Patterns of socially acceptable behaviour and underlying values and belief systems are communicated, sometimes blatantly in the form of punishment or rewards, but more often subtly through adult models of behaviour, games, stories and everyday experiences. A child's emerging *identity* is constructed in relation to the social groups to which she belongs. She learns that certain behaviour and language is appropriate with peers, but not with older relatives; she understands that moods and images which evoke a response within the home are not productive at school. With maturity, she develops a range of identities to suit the various social contexts which she inhabits.

Childhood is the critical phase in the formation of an individual's identity. From outside come the exhortations of society to behave, believe, think and feel according to what is regarded as 'normal'; from within come the primal urges emanating from a unique blend of human attributes. 'On the one hand *socialization* means the "transmission of the culture", the particular culture an individual enters at birth; on the other hand the term is used to mean the "process of becoming human", in acquiring uniquely human attributes from interaction with others' (Wrong, 1972, p. 53). The resulting dynamic interplay between self and society – for some a harmonious experience, for others a process of anguish and bitterness – characterizes the period of childhood in all cultures.

The realization that perceptions of, and attitudes towards, childhood vary from one culture to another can be profoundly liberating, for both children and adults. Understanding that childhood – a universal condition – is not subject to universal laws, aspirations or codes of conduct provides a handy entry point into the conceptual maze of perspective consciousness; through a fusion of personal experience and wider knowledge, students can begin to perceive childhood as, at the same time, unique and universal.

Initiation

Initiation was the most important event in Aboriginal life, one of the special times when the whole tribe gathered in a season of plenty to celebrate and perpetuate the Dreamtime. Both boys and girls were initiated in sacred rituals which celebrated their passage into adulthood and which were integral to the special roles they would have as men and women within tribal society. Boys were initiated at about the age of thirteen.

Much more is known about male initiation in New South Wales, mainly because early anthropologists were men and talked to men. The making of the young men seems to have been a more public event in the life of the tribe, but the initiation of girls was also integral to ceremonial life.

At the appointed time the whole tribe, often with neighbouring tribes, would gather at the Bora ground. 'Bora' is a Kamilaroy word meaning belt of manhood, the loin cloth girdle worn by initiated men. Bora grounds consisted of two cleared rings – a larger public space and a smaller secret ceremonial place, roughly 30 metres and 15 metres in diameter – connected by a pathway running east to west, symbolizing the progress of life. In and around the rings, especially the smaller secret place, and along the connecting track, were Dreamtime images, carved trees, rock carvings, paintings and earth sculptures of Baiame, totem ancestors, the sun, moon and stars.

For both boys and girls the final ceremonies were the climax of a lifetime of education which became particularly intensive in the final stages. Boys, for example, were told to keep their mouths shut, listen to the old men and learn. A vast amount of Dreamtime knowledge of land, people and law was needed to become a full member of Aboriginal society.

More than knowledge was needed to become a man. Boys were subject to rigorous tests of self-discipline, such as lying in the one place with eyes closed, not moving or speaking for days at a time. During the final ceremonies, tribes around Sydney would knock out one of the front teeth, and many tribes performed the symbolic rite of circumcision with a sharp stone. In all areas the chest, arms and back were ritually scarred to produce the markings of a man. The scars of initiation were, and are, worn with pride.

Initiations lasted several days with public and secret ceremonies. These began at the outer circle of the Bora ground when the voice of the Bull Roarer was heard. The Bull Roarer was the voice of Baiame. It was a flat disc of stone with holes bored through it, attached to a fibre rope. When swung around the head it made a noise like thunder or a bull bellowing.

With possum skin rugs over their heads, the boys were taken away to the sacred inner circle. They were painted white, symbolizing both the death of children and the birth of men. At the secret place they were shown the sacred tjuringa and the totems of all the clans.

When the boys finally returned to the group as men, they were given their proper weapons and sent out to live off the land. After their return they lived in a special section of the camp and continued their education under the supervision of the Elders.

The 1989 Convention on the Rights of the Child defines a child as 'every human being below the age of 18 years unless, under the law applicable to the child, majority is attained earlier' (Part 1, Article 1). The difficulties inherent in reaching a universally acceptable definition of childhood – amongst adults, let alone children – are bound up in varying cultural perspectives on the legal age at which young people are mature enough to break free from the protection and restriction of child laws and the influence of parents or guardians. In Turkey, for example, individuals may marry, leave home and be conscripted at 18, but not stand for Parliament until they attain the age of 30; in Japan, young people can marry with parental consent at 16 but may not vote or drink alcohol under 20 years of age. These examples illustrate the dilemma of using terms like 'childhood', as in different societies, and in different historical periods, the process of maturation is recognized and labelled in various ways. For the sake of convenience and brevity, the 1989 Convention definition of childhood is used throughout this book.

Some societies clearly identify stages of acceptance into full adulthood. Prior to the European invasion of Australia, most Aboriginal groups inducted boys and girls into adult roles and religious knowledge through a series of initiation ceremonies, like that described in New South Wales in the extract opposite (Parbury, 1986, p. 2).

As societies undergo industrialization, however, ritual celebration of the transition from childhood to adulthood decreases in significance. The *rites of passage* still exist but, like leaving school or home, they do not affect everyone of a similar age or, like the acquisition of a driving licence, do not involve the entire community in ritual recognition of new roles and responsibilities. Furthermore, the powers and privileges of adult status are conferred gradually over a period of time rather than at one socially sanctioned ceremony.

Cultural interpretations of childhood, and the *childrearing* practices to which they lead, are designed to assist children to adapt, as painlessly as possible, to the adult environment in which they grow. In native Australian and American communities in pre-European times children were encouraged to be co-operative and observant and to develop the skills needed in foraging for plants, hunting and supervising younger siblings – attributes that are essential in hunter–gatherer societies. In industrialized countries the demand for a technologically sophisticated workforce has given rise to extensive compulsory schooling and, consequently, a lengthy period of economic dependence upon parents.

Understanding the cultural context is vital to an appreciation of different childrearing practices. As American anthropologist Wendy Schottman discovered when she took her 14-month-old daughter Iza to Baatombu in Benin, having one's own values and beliefs challenged from a different *cultural perspective* can be an uncomfortable experience (Schottman, 1988, p. 11).

July 4th

No doubt because she didn't have a nap, Iza was particularly annoying yesterday at dinner. I served her yam, but she didn't want that. She pointed to something on the table and said 'eh!' I picked up one thing after another trying to identify her desire. It turned out to be peanut butter, which I know she doesn't like. I gave her a spoonful anyway. She rejected it and screamed louder. I offered her my breast. That wasn't what she wanted. I put her back in her highchair with the bowl of yams. She pushed it angrily away. I caught it, then slapped her and turned, my nerves completely frizzled, to eat my dinner.

I suspect that Iza's saviours had already entered before I slapped her, but the darkness allowed me to ignore them. Now they crowded around with the first, oldest, wife of the older brother up front which is always bad news. She said she had seen me hit Iza, that one doesn't hit a child, that Iza was crying and wanted a nurse. I said no, that she had refused to nurse. 'Wesa!' (That's not true!) she shouted and I had to pick Iza up from where she was having a tantrum on the floor to show them how she refused my breast. 'She wants to eat! Give her food.' 'She doesn't want to eat. She refused. She threw it on the floor!' 'Give it to her!' So I picked Iza up and shoved her into her chair and gave her the bowl. She pushed it away violently and everyone saw. 'She doesn't know what she wants,' I said. 'She wants to scream.' I turned back to my dinner and they hung around a minute at a loss for words or maybe just amazed by Iza's behaviour and then they left.

I was a bit shaken. Sometimes I wonder why I behave like I do with Iza. Why I reason as I do. It's a very uncomfortable feeling. There are so many beliefs and values we have that we are hardly aware of them because they are shared by all those around us, completely evident, never challenged. Now I sometimes feel stripped, painfully aware of all these beliefs and guidelines, painfully aware of their arbitrariness.

Wendy Schottman's actions reflected the assumption held by many in the West that a child's behaviour must be consciously shaped by punishment and reward to ensure her proper development: 'as the twig is bent so grows the tree.' As Lee Comer points out, however, other societies, unburdened by the gurus of child psychology, believe that child development is principally a natural process. 'When children are not regarded as a separate sub-species with special needs and requirements, that society will not have opinions about how children will be reared. Children merely are, and instead of being brought up they grow up . . . Where children of our own past (and in other societies now) took profound responsibilities, perhaps for a herd of goats, or for the care of their younger siblings, children of the same age in our society can barely tie their shoelaces. The first and hardest lesson is that children are not special, vulnerable, defenceless and incapable and easily traumatized. The fact that they appear so is because we have made them so' (Comer, 1979, pp. 154–5).

In industrialized societies deliberate and calculated intervention in the process of maturation is at the core of educational thinking and practice, whether this be achieved through the formal transmission of knowledge and beliefs in the classroom or, more subtly, through providing the child with appropriate objects and experiences at home. 'Even when children [in Japan] are left to play alone, they are these days often surrounded by "educational" toys, or a conveniently placed pile of sand or dirt, since these are also thought to be "good" for the child . . . . Kindergarten teachers take great pains to teach children arts such as origami and calligraphy, not only by demonstration but, where necessary, by guiding a child's fingers in the correct motions' (Hendry, 1982, p. 70). Wilfred Pelletier's reminiscence of his native American childhood recalls a rather different relationship to teachers and teaching (Pelletier, 1972, pp. 58–9).

One of the very important things was the relationship we had with our families. We didn't always live at home. We lived wherever we happened to be at that particular time when it got dark. If you were two or three miles away from home, then that is where you slept. People would feed you even if they didn't know who you were. We'd spend an evening, perhaps with an old couple, and they would tell us stories. Most of these stories were legends, and they were told to us mostly in the winter time. In the summer people would generally take us out and we would do a number of things which in some way would allow us to learn about life and what it was all about: that is, by talking about some particular person and demonstrating what the person did. At no time, in all the years I spent there, do I ever remember anyone teaching us anything.

These things I remember very well. We were brought up to have a different relationship to a house and to all the things that surrounded us. That is, the values that adults placed on things in the community did not necessarily carry over into their child and lead him to place the same values on them. Children discovered the values of these things on their own, and developed their own particular relationship to them.

2. Children's rights

In 1979 the United Nations Commission on Human Rights set up a Working Group to draft a comprehensive international document on *children's rights*; a document which would transcend cultural differences and be applicable to children in every society in the world.

The Working Group, consisting of representatives from 43 UN member states, found the task a formidable one. They found significantly divergent perceptions from one country to another regarding the age at which childhood ends and the child's economic role in the family and society begins. They found methods of upbringing and socialization that varied greatly. The development of an unambiguous document that could be applied to situations as diverse as child victims of warfare in Nicaragua, Vietnamese refugees in Hong Kong and Muslim girls wishing to wear headscarves to school in Paris, provided a great challenge.

The Convention on the Rights of the Child (adopted by the UN General Assembly in November 1989) was the outcome of a decade of deliberations by the Working Group, supported by UN organizations, especially UNICEF, and the global community of non-governmental organizations. It is a long document of 54 articles and is much more detailed and thoroughgoing than the UN Declaration of the Rights of the Child of 1959. A summary of the rights laid down in the Convention appears on pp. 6–7. Copies in English and also French and Spanish (useful resources for language teachers) are available from UNICEF. The document marks a significant step forward in the identification of universally-held cultural values. In reiterating the essential point that certain values are fundamental and inalienable whatever the state of the world, it has helped compound global acceptance of those values. 'The Convention matters not least because it exists, because never again will it be possible to draft a law about children without referring to it' (Moorhead, 1989).

One way of categorizing the rights enshrined in the Convention is to see them as being concerned with *development* and *provision* (i.e. ensuring optimum conditions for the development of a child's potential), *protection* (i.e. providing freedom from abuse, exploitation, cruelty, injustice and neglect) and *participation* (i.e. offering children the chance to express opinions, to have a say in matters affecting their lives and to play an active role in society). Another is to decide whether the rights laid down are civil and political rights or social and economic rights. The former (sometimes referred to as liberty-oriented rights) are rights concerned with giving individuals freedom of action and choice and freedom to participate in political and other decision-making processes. The latter (sometimes referred to as security-oriented rights) seek to protect people's physical, material, social and economic well-being. Whatever mode of classification is used, it will soon become clear that the categories, although helpful in building a conceptual understanding of rights, are by no means watertight. Protection, for example, embraces much of what is implied by development and the right to participation is essential both for achieving optimal development and for ensuring maximum protection.

The Convention required ratification by 20 UN member states before it became binding on those states and upon other states which subsequently ratified its provisions. August 1990 saw the number of ratifying states rise above 20 and in early September 1990 the Convention entered into force. By the end of February 1991 the number of ratifying states had risen to 75. The United Kingdom ratified the Convention on 16 December 1991. By September 1997 ratifying states numbered 191.

Many of the rights laid down in the Convention are enshrined in UK law. They can, thus, be claimed by children as their *legal rights* over and above their claim to those rights on grounds of general principles of morality, fairness and justice (the claim to moral rights).

Summary of the Convention on the Rights of the Child

The Convention defines a child as a person under 18 unless national law recognizes that the age of majority is reached earlier (Article 1). All the rights laid down in the Convention are to be enjoyed by children regardless of race, colour, sex, language, religion, political or other opinion, national, ethnic or social origin, property, disability, birth or other status (Article 2).

Every child has:

The right to life (Article 6).

The right to an identity, i.e. the right to a name, the right to a nationality and, as far as possible, the right to know her/his parents and to be cared for by them (Article 7).

The right to live with her/his parents unless incompatible with her/his best interests (Article 9).

The right to maintain personal relations and direct contact with both parents if separated from one or both unless incompatible with her/his best interests (Article 9).

The right to leave and enter her/his own country, and other countries, for purposes of reunion with parents and maintaining the child–parent relationship (Article 10).

The right to freely express an opinion in all matters affecting her/him and to have that opinion given due weight in accordance with age and maturity (Article 12).

The right to express views and transmit ideas and information to others through the media of her/his choice (Article 13).

The right to freedom of thought, conscience and religion, subject to parental guidance of a kind appropriate to her/his age and capacities (Article 14).

The right to meet together with other children and join and form associations (Article 15).

The right to protection from arbitrary and unlawful interference with privacy, family, home and correspondence, and from libel and slander (Article 16).

The right of access to information and materials from a diversity of sources and of protection from harmful materials (Article 17).

The right to benefit from childrearing assistance and child-care services and facilities provided to parents/guardians by the state (Article 18).

The right to protection from maltreatment by parents or others responsible for her/his care (Article 19).

The right to special protection if s/he is temporarily or permanently deprived of her/his family environment, due regard being paid to her/his cultural background (Article 20).

The right in countries where adoption is allowed, to have it ensured that an adoption is carried out in her/his best interests (Article 21).

The right, if a refugee, to special protection (Article 22).

The right, if disabled, to special care, education and training to help her/him enjoy a full and decent life in conditions which ensure dignity, which promote self-reliance and which maximize the opportunities for participation and integration in society (Article 23).

The right to the highest standard of health and medical care attainable (Article 24).

The right, if placed by the state for purposes of care, protection or treatment, to have all aspects of that placement regularly evaluated (Article 25).

The right to benefit from social security, including social insurance (Article 26).

The right to a standard of living adequate for her/his physical, mental, spiritual, moral and social development (Article 27).

The right to education, including free primary education (Article 28).

The right, if a member of a minority community or indigenous people, to enjoy her/his own culture, to practise her/his own religion and use her/his own language (Article 30).

The right to rest and leisure, to engage in play and to participate in recreational, cultural and artistic activities (Article 31).

The right to protection from economic exploitation and work that is hazardous, interferes with her/his education or harms her/his health or physical, mental, spiritual, moral and social development (Article 32).

The right to protection from narcotic drugs and from being involved in their production or distribution (Article 33).

The right to protection from sexual exploitation and abuse (Article 34).

The right to protection from being abducted, sold or trafficked (Article 35).

The right to protection from all other forms of exploitation (Article 36).

The right not to be subjected to torture or other cruel, inhuman or degrading treatment or punishment (Article 37).

The right, if below 18 years of age, not to be sentenced to capital punishment or imprisonment (without the possibility of release) for offences committed (Article 37).

The right, if deprived of liberty for offences committed, to prompt access to legal and other appropriate assistance, to separation from adult prisoners and to contact with family (Article 37).

The right, if below 15 years of age, not to be recruited into armed forces nor to engage in direct hostilities (Article 38).

The right, if the victim of armed conflict, torture, neglect, maltreatment or exploitation, to receive appropriate treatment for her/his physical and psychological recovery and reintegration into society (Article 39).

The right, if accused or guilty of committing an offence, to age-appropriate treatment likely to promote her/his sense of dignity and worth and her/his reintegration as a constructive member of society (Article 40).

The right to be informed of these principles and provisions by the state in which s/he lives (Article 42).

Note: The above is an article-by-article summary of the rights of the child as laid down in the Convention. The Convention has 54 Articles in all. Articles 42 to 54 are concerned with its implementation and entry into force.

The Convention on the Rights of the Child was adopted by the United Nations General Assembly 20 November 1989.

In both ratifying and non-ratifying states, children's enjoyment of rights remains variable, haphazard and incomplete. *Rights denials* and *violations* are tolerated by societies in all parts of the world. Children experience *discrimination* on grounds of ethnicity, race, gender, disability and socio-economic status. *Child abuse* and *harassment*, especially the sexual harassment of girls, came to public attention as significant social issues during the 1980s. *Child labour* and *child exploitation* (economic, sexual) are smouldering issues that have burst into increasing prominence in the 1990s.

In 1948 the Universal Declaration of Human Rights asserted that 'everyone has a right to education'. In 1959 the UN Declaration of the Rights of the Child included 'the right to free education'. The 1989 Convention on the Rights of the Child recognizes 'the right of the child to education' and signatory nations are asked to 'make primary education compulsory and available free to all' and to make secondary education available and accessible. These documents notwithstanding, the World Conference on Education for All, meeting in Thailand from 5 to 9 March 1990, noted that more than 100 million children, including at least 60 million girls, have no access to even primary schooling. The question of *learning entitlement* (i.e. entitlement to education and to appropriate learning) is, thus, central to any serious consideration of children's rights.

For those children who are at school the question remains as to whether the curriculum is appropriate for adult life in the twenty-first century. Is it so designed to develop 'personality, talents and mental and physical abilities to their fullest potential', 'respect for human rights and fundamental freedoms' and 'respect for the natural environment' (Convention, Article 29)? Does the 'respect for human rights and fundamental freedoms' manifest itself in recognition of *student rights* as well as *responsibilities* within the school? Do schools 'assure to the child who is capable of forming his or her own views the right to express those views freely in all matters affecting the child'? Do they provide children with 'the opportunity to be heard in any judicial and administrative proceedings' affecting their interests, and the swift and effective handling of *rights denials* and *violations* (Convention, Article 12)?

One way in which schools can enable children to express their views in matters affecting them and, at the same time, provide valuable practice in democratic and participatory citizenship (see section 3) is to give scope for students to undertake *campaigning* and *action* programmes using the classroom as a springboard. A powerful example of what is possible has been provided by the Norwegian-based Voice of the Children International Campaign. Following the meeting of the World Commission on Environment and Development, held in Bergen, Norway, in May 1990, ten Norwegian children were given the opportunity to put their hopes, fears, demands and visions for the world's future to their country's leaders at a children's hearing. The hearing, which received widespread media coverage in Norway, was the culmination of a process which had started with letters to schools inviting students to send postcards conveying their thoughts and feelings about the state of the world's environment and world development. Some 6000 postcards were received. An editing group clustered the cards under a number of headings and drew up a Children's Appeal reflecting the children's opinions and using the children's own words.

At the hearing, the ten selected children put questions to a panel which included the then Norwegian prime minister, Gro Harlem Brundtland, and other national figures. The Norwegian Children's Ombudsman chaired the hearing and ensured that questions were answered without evasion. After the hearing, the Appeal was presented to the media, non-governmental organizations, and schools. Looking back on the event, Gro Harlem Brundtland wrote:

> I believe this was an important event – for the children who were invited to take
> part in the political process at a very high level, for the political leadership who had
> to face the challenges from the children taking part, and for the children and
> grown-ups in the audience who became part of the process. We need engaged,
> informed, active young people. We need young people who believe they can be part

of the process, who have enough faith and enough self-confidence to fight for their future and the future of the world.

The Voice of the Children International Campaign is now promoting children's hearings at school, local, regional, national and global levels (a global children's hearing was held in Rio de Janeiro during the Earth Summit in June 1992 with children from all parts of the world). Activity 21 gives guidance on organizing a school-based hearing and ideas for student involvement in decision-making and opinion-forming processes are offered at various points in this book.

Interestingly, and importantly, world leaders meeting at the World Summit for Children in New York on 30 September 1990 added their voice to the call to children to play their part in confronting poverty, environmental degradation and the scourge of war. 'Among the partnerships we seek, we turn especially to children', they declared. 'We appeal to them to participate in the effort' (*World Declaration on the Survival, Protection and Development of Children*, Clause 22). In an opening statement, the Co-President of the World Summit, Brian Mulroney, then Prime Minister of Canada, spoke directly to children. 'It is your generation that will eventually judge how well we have understood your own special problems. And it is you who will hold us to account for our efforts to resolve them. . . . To the children who are here today – and to those who are listening – I say I invite you to listen carefully to what we say and, in the coming years, *to hold us to our commitments*. I hope that none of us will be found wanting' (our italics).

The fact that the Gulf War, fought at an horrendous cost to children, followed hard on the heels of the World Summit encourages cynicism about the value of lofty statements on the rights of the child. The monitoring machinery established under the Convention, with its potential for shaping opinion and embarrassing governments (reports from signatory states are to be made 'widely available'), will be crucial in the middle and long term.

Rigorous monitoring can, however, drive human rights abuses underground. Researching into child labour in Naples, Goddard found instances where the enforcement of child labour regulations had disastrous implications for child workers. Economic necessity forced children as young as ten to look for work in clothing and shoe factories. Large 'respectable' factories refused to employ them, fearing prosecution from industrial inspectors; so children were forced to accept work in small, unsafe, semi-secret factories where conditions were not monitored. In a Casvatore workshop in 1976, three girls were killed in a fire because all exits were blocked by machinery and stock (Goddard, 1985, p. 20).

Interpreting statements of rights to determine the best interests of the child is a complex affair, not least because of the potential contradictions and tensions that exist between the rights laid down. Article 32 of the Convention recognizes the right of children to be protected from work that is exploitative or hazardous in nature, that interferes with their education and threatens their health and development. But what if the money earned by the child is an essential contribution to the family income, and thus to any hope of her realizing her right to an adequate standard of living (Article 27)? And what if she regards formal education, along with increasing numbers of children in the developed world, as an irrelevance? What if, from her perspective, adequately paid employment offers an alternative to schooling that better fosters the development of her personality, talents and mental and physical abilities (Article 29)? To what extent does her right to have her opinions given due weight (Article 12) come into play? And where there is a conflict between the rights enshrined in the Convention, how should priorities be determined and claims weighed, and who should make the decisions?

Concern has been expressed that the Convention fails to address the *causes* of child neglect and abuse globally. In 1989 there were 17 countries with an under-five mortality rate of over 20 per cent and some 51 countries with a rate of 10 per cent or over (Grant, 1991, p. 102). During 1987 the 95 low- and middle-income developing countries spent an average 1.1 per cent of Gross Domestic Product on health expenditure, 2.5 per cent on education expenditure and 4.5 per cent on servicing their debt to banks in the rich world

(Grant, 1991, p. 13). In 1990 there were 177 million malnourished under-fives in the developing world. Despite their regions' food surpluses, 47 per cent of under-fives in South Asia and 14 per cent in Latin America lacked adequate

---

CHILDREN'S APPEAL TO WORLD LEADERS, RIO DE JANEIRO, JUNE 1992

WE WANT TO INHERIT A CLEAN EARTH.

We would like everybody to understand that the Earth is like a beautiful garden in which no one has the right to destroy anything.
We would like our grandchildren to know: What is a tree, a fish, a dog. Leave us trees to climb in.

ECOLOGY IS NOT JUST TREES, ANIMALS AND RIVERS, IT IS ALSO HUNGER AND THE HOMELESS.

We should all help our brothers and sisters who have been abandoned on the streets. Eliminate poverty.
We want you to understand that all excessive consumption affects developing countries most.

WE WANT CHILDREN'S RIGHTS TO BE RESPECTED ALL OVER THE WORLD.

No child should be imprisoned or beaten, no child should die of hunger or from diseases that could easily be prevented. All children have a right to have parents.

WE WANT EVERY GIRL AND BOY IN THE WORLD TO GET AN EDUCATION FOR A BETTER START IN LIFE.
WE WANT TO SEE ILLITERACY WIPED OUT.

It is our future and we want to have a say in it. We want to be educated in such a way that we get the courage to speak our minds. We want a world without discrimination.

WE WANT VERY STRICT LAWS AGAINST DESTROYING NATURE.

Anybody polluting the environment should have to pay large fines.
Stop producing materials that harm the ozone layer or it will be broken and the sun's rays will burn us. Stop global warming, reduce CO_2 emissions. Cut the use of fossil fuels, use sun and wind power. Instead of drilling for more oil, use energy less wastefully.

WE WANT YOU TO STOP USING NUCLEAR POWER.

End nuclear testing in our oceans and seas, we demand the removal of all nuclear power stations.

WE DON'T WANT OUR CITIES TO BE RUINED BY CARS.

We don't want to be sick from exhaust fumes. We want you to make cars that don't pollute. Public transportation should be better, cheaper and more efficient than private cars. Make it easier for us all to use our bicycles.

WE DON'T WANT OUR WORLD TO DROWN IN RUBBISH.
NOBODY SHOULD BE ALLOWED TO DUMP THEIR RUBBISH IN OTHER COUNTRIES.

Stop littering, make less waste. We don't need all the packaging materials.

WE WOULD LIKE ALL THINGS TO BE RECYCLED.

Make it easier for people to recycle their rubbish.
Stop producing disposables.

PLEASE, LEADERS OF THE WORLD, GIVE US CLEAN DRINKING WATER.

Without water there is no life. Too many children are drinking clayish water from shallow wells, pipe borne water is still a luxury. Too many children spend hours walking a long way to find water.

WE FEAR THAT WHEN WE GROW UP THERE WILL BE NO
FISH IN THE OCEAN.

We want you to stop oil spills in the oceans, to stop factories from releasing their sewage and waste into rivers and lakes. The sea cannot absorb poison without being harmed.

ANIMALS HAVE AS MUCH RIGHT TO LIVE ON THIS EARTH AS WE DO.

Protect endangered animals, stop buying products made from rare animals. People should be able to do without real fur coats, crocodile leather or jewelry from ivory. Ban animal testing for cosmetics, ban killing animals for sport.

WE WANT MORE DONE TO SAVE WHAT IS LEFT OF THE NATIVE FORESTS.

The rainforests are home to many people and animals. We want indigenous peoples to be able to live by their own rules. Don't cut down all the native trees because the birds need homes, just like all the children in the world.

WE ARE AFRAID OF BEING SWEPT OFF THE FACE OF OUR COUNTRY BY THE APPROACHING DESERT.

Stop bush-burning and overgrazing that is killing our trees and hurting our grassland vegetation. We want canals to be built alongside the main rivers to prevent flooding. Stop building large dams against people's wishes.

ALL HAVE A RIGHT TO LIVE IN PEACE.

The money spent on military armaments should be spent on saving the planet. Instead of making bombs, improve the standard of living in the world.

THE EARTH IS A SINGLE COUNTRY, AND ALL PEOPLE ARE ITS CITIZENS.

We have to share this planet, so don't be selfish. We want food to be shared so that everyone has enough. We want clean water and a home for all people. We are worried about pollution, war and children starving, while others don't appreciate the food they get. We are afraid that the world will soon belong only to the rich.

**THIS EARTH IS MORE VALUABLE THAN ALL THE MONEY IN THE WORLD.
WE WANT ALL COUNTRIES TO WORK TOGETHER TO PROTECT IT.**

nourishment (Grant, 1991, p. 29). The problem here is not the absence of an international statement of children's rights but the existence of a global economic order unfairly tilted against the developing world, in which children's lives have been mortgaged through cuts in education, health care, services and subsidies to make huge debt repayments to banks in the West. 'Children have suffered first and most, not last and least' (Grant, 1991, p. 28). In acknowledgement of this, world leaders at the World Summit for Children enunciated a new ethic for children in their Plan of Action – the principle of 'first call for children'. 'First call' recognizes that 'the essential needs of children should be given high priority in the allocation of resources, in bad times as well as in good times, at national and international as well as at family levels' (Grant, 1991, p. 69). It remains to be seen whether the governments and financial institutions of the world embrace the new ethic and critically review and act upon some of the entrenched causes of child poverty and abuse, such as the global trade in arms, prices paid by the rich for the products of the developing world, and debt repayments. The ultimate impact of the Convention is bound up in a broad strategy for ensuring children a better future that necessarily addresses such issues.

> The need for that new ethic arises, as ethics usually do, from practical as well as moral roots. The special vulnerability and the special responsiveness of the early years, demand that the child's one chance for normal growth should be given a first call on our concerns and capacities.
>
> Those same reasons also demand that children should be able to count on the commitment in good times and in bad – in lean times and in times of plenty, in times of peace and in times of war, in times of recession or in times of steadily advancing prosperity. The mental and physical growth of a child cannot be asked to wait until interest rates fall, or until commodity prices recover, or until debt repayments have been rescheduled, or until the economy returns to growth, or until after a general election, or until a war is over. The ethic of first call for children does not demand that protection for the lives and the development of the young should be a priority; it demands that it should be an absolute. It does not demand the kind of commitment which can be superseded by other priorities that suddenly seem more urgent, but the kind of commitment that will not waver in the winds of change which will always blow across the world of human affairs.
>
> There will always be something more immediate. There will never be anything more important.
>
> James Grant, Executive Director of UNICEF
> (Grant, 1991, p. 27)

3. Education for citizenship

The Convention requires ratifying states to make its provisions 'widely known, by appropriate and active means, to adults and children alike' (Article 42). The United Kingdom has identified the Convention as a topic for study, within education for citizenship, one of the five cross-curricular themes of the National Curriculum for England and Wales. This book offers an approach to citizenship that focuses on something of which all students have direct, immediate and vivid experience: childhood.

In *Curriculum Guidance 8* the then National Curriculum Council made the crucially important point that the ethos of both classroom and school is central to effective citizenship: education for democratic rights-respectful and participative citizenship within a pluralist society and interdependent world calls for a learning climate that promotes self-esteem, mutual respect, tolerance of difference, open-mindedness and participation. It is, at best, characterized by relationships and processes that exhibit an intrinsic respect for the rights (whilst, of course, reaffirming the responsibilities) of students and teachers. It is also marked by the availability of opportunities for democratic empowerment whether through group decision-making, joint negotiation of the curriculum or involvement in forms of *action, campaigning* and *change agency* around students' concerns within and beyond the school walls (NCC, 1990, pp. 4, 10, 15). 'Democracy is best learned in a democratic setting where participation is encouraged, where views can be expressed openly and discussed, where there is freedom of expression for pupils and teachers, and where there is fairness and justice. An appropriate climate is, therefore, an essential complement to effective learning about human rights' (Council of Europe, 1985, Appendix, para. 4.1).

The 21 activities in this book accordingly set great store upon learning that is *experiential, interactive* and *participatory* and that involves perspective sharing, consensus seeking and decision making. A diversity of learning approaches is offered in recognition that different students learn best in different ways and that learning style monoculture is a denial of equality of opportunity. There are various activities, too, that, in part or whole, offer action, campaigning and change agency opportunities.

References

Comer, L. (1979) In M. Hoyles (ed.) *Changing Childhood*. London: Writers and
    Readers.
Council of Europe (1985) *Recommendation no. R(85)7 of the Committee of Ministers to
    Member States on Teaching and Learning about Human Rights in Schools*.
Goddard, V. (1985) 'Child labour in Naples', *Anthropology Today* **1** (5).
Grant, J. P. (1991) *The State of the World's Children 1991*. Oxford: Oxford University
    Press.
Hendry, J. (1982) 'Teaching about children with ethnographic material', *Social Science
    Teacher* **11** (3).
Moorhead, C. (1989) 'United against the horrors that face the world's children', *The
    Independent*, 24 October 1989.
National Curriculum Council (1990) *Curriculum Guidance 8: Education for Citizenship*.
Parbury, N. (1986) *Survival: A History of Aboriginal Life in New South Wales*. Sydney:
    Ministry of Aboriginal Affairs.
Pelletier, W. (1972) 'Childhood in an Indian village'. In D. Jay (ed.), *The American
    Indian: The First Victim*. New York: William Morrow.
Schottman, W. (1988) 'Participant, observer and mother in an African village',
    Anthropology Today **4** (2).
Wrong, D. (1972) In D. Weeks, *A Glossary of Sociological Concepts*. Milton Keynes:
    Open University Press.

ACTIVITY 1
Affirmation consequences

Time needed	20 minutes.
Resources	A sheet of plain A4 paper and a pen for each student.
Procedure	Sitting in circles of six to eight people, each student writes her name at the bottom of the sheet of paper and passes it to her neighbour. Students are then asked to write an affirming statement about the person whose name appears on the sheet. The statement can be about character, abilities, appearance or any other personal attribute, and can be of any length from one word to a full sentence; it must, however, be positive and affirming. After writing the statement, students fold down the top of the sheet to cover the comment. The sheet is passed to the next person in the circle and the process is repeated until each student has written on all the sheets. After reading the affirmative statements about herself, each student in turn reads out these statements to the group, using the 'I' form, e.g. 'I am good at maths', 'I have kind eyes', 'I am a special friend'.
Potential	An emotionally-charged activity which can clearly reveal peer group opinions and perspectives on oneself, by what is *not* said as well as from the actual comments. It should only be attempted with a group of students who know each other well and can be trusted to write affirmative comments. Class discussion following the activity could focus on the participants' feelings at the various stages of the activity. Many people find it difficult to say affirmative things to each other. Why is this? Does writing them secretly help? How did it feel to receive all these positive comments? How did it feel to read them out? Do class members feel that their culture encourages them to think and say positive things about themselves? Are there other situations when students remember the impact of affirmative statements or, conversely, the effect of not receiving them or of receiving negative statements? Students might also be invited to reflect upon any statements about themselves they find surprising and any general difference between their own and others' perception of themselves.
Variation	Before starting the activity students are asked to write down, on a separate sheet of paper, six to eight affirmative statements about themselves. This sheet is put away whilst the activity proceeds and later used as a comparison with the image presented to each student by her peers.
Source	Various.

ACTIVITY 2
MEtaphor

Time needed   25 minutes.

Resources   The five metaphors below, displayed so that everyone can see them; sheet of paper and pen for each student.

Procedure   Students brainstorm, as a whole class, the factors which they believe shape individual identity (e.g. names, family upbringing, peer influences, childhood success/failure). Students then reflect individually on the following metaphors and decide which are the two most apposite to describe how they believe their own identity and character is formed. In pairs, they discuss

---

My identity is like:

dough – other people (family, friends, teachers) shape and mould me

a plant – within me there is the potential for flowering, if the growing conditions are right

a train timetable – everything is clearly laid down in theory, but in reality is subject to change, re-routing and delay.

a large computer – I have the potential for amazing things, if only I can learn how it operates

an artist's canvas – what I become depends upon how I use the brushes and colours

---

the two they have chosen and then try to think of other appropriate MEtaphors to describe their identities. A class list of MEtaphors is compiled and displayed.

Potential   A creative thinking activity which encourages students to explore complex questions concerning their identity and how it is formed. Follow-up discussion could focus on the nature versus nurture debate (i.e. to what extent our identity is shaped biologically and to what extent by social and environmental forces).

ACTIVITY 3
Identity auction

Time needed	30 minutes.
Resources	A worksheet of items for sale for each student; a hammer or shoe.
Procedure	Worksheets are handed out and each student is given an imaginary 1000 units of currency to bid for and buy desired items on the list. Time having been given for everybody to study the list and choose preferred items, the auction begins in a brisk, lively style. Items are sold to the individual bidding the most (the deal is sealed when the hammer or shoe is banged on the table). The auctioneer – teacher or student – takes cues from students as to what item to auction as well as choosing items herself. Students can put up three items of their own choosing for auction (to be added to the list in spaces 28–30). They should keep a careful record of account by filling in the balance sheet provided.
Potential	This activity encourages students to identify those personal attributes they value most and to assess the attributes valued by others. Follow-up discussion can begin by asking students to explain what they bought, why they were keen to buy those items and also to identify items they would have liked but were unable to purchase. Then discussion could look at:

The 'auction effect'. If something seems to be in demand, why do others start wanting it too? What examples of the 'auction effect' have students noted in everyday life?

Individual differences. Did the auction help students learn something about themselves and about others taking part? Did it provide a context and opportunity for students to express their own individuality, their hopes and aspirations?

Communication. Did students find it easier to say certain things about themselves in an auction context which would normally have been difficult to say? Can they think of other kinds of situations which help to make communication easier (e.g. romantic evenings, parties, writing letters rather than telling someone directly)?

Extension	With some background information about young people in other societies (see, for example, the case studies in Activity 13), students attempt to empathize with another person in a different situation and bid for appropriate items from the other's perspective.
Source	Based on an activity in D. Wolsk, *An Experience-centered Curriculum*, Educational Studies and Documents No. 17. Paris: UNESCO, 1974.

Identity Auction
Items for sale

1. All-round sporting ability
2. Ability to make a few close friends
3. Happy family life
4. Ability to lead others
5. Artistic skills and success
6. Love of learning
7. Good health
8. Chances for adventure
9. Lots of money
10. Ability to do very well in school
11. Success in the job of your choice
12. Good looks
13. Ability to do practical things
14. Feeling important
15. Musical talent
16. Ability to bounce back
17. Ability to give love to others
18. Ability to help other people
19. Ability to make lots of friends
20. Success at changing the world to make it a better place
21. Parents who trust you
22. A secure and safe future
23. The chance to travel wherever you want
24. Real excellence in one sport
25. Feeling really good about yourself
26. Ability to read well
27. Ability to speak out in class or in public
28.
29.
30.

Units of money at start of auction:		
Item no.	Price paid	Balance

ACTIVITY 4
What is a child?

Time needed	Two hours or several lessons.
Resources	Rough paper for each pair of students; two sheets of chart paper for each group of six; felt-tip pens.
Procedure	*Stage 1: What is a child?* Students form pairs and brainstorm responses to the question 'What is a child?' Any response is accepted and students are encouraged to write down as many as possible. Pairs then come together in groups of six to discuss and negotiate composite lists (avoiding duplication) which are written up on chart paper. Responses can be rejected if the group agrees they are not valid; the remaining responses should be written up in clusters of similar ideas, where possible. Finally, groups meet each other briefly to share what they have produced (40 minutes).

Stage 2: What is a (British) child?

The procedure described above is again followed (different pairs can be formed), the question this time being 'What is a (name of student's own nationality) child, which distinguishes her from a child of another nationality?' Ideally, but not necessarily, groups should be composed of students of the same nationality (40 minutes).

Stage 3: Who am I?

Students work individually, listing on a sheet of paper as many things they can think of which distinguish them as individuals from all other individuals. They mark an X on the top of their paper if they are prepared to permit the facilitator to read items from the list so that other students can try to guess their identity. (20 minutes)

Potential

The exercises above, which should each be followed by class plenary discussion, are concerned with major aspects of identity as human beings and as children. An increasing degree of difficulty is generally encountered as students progress through the three stages.

What is a child? seeks to determine those characteristics universally shared by children and which set them apart from adults (and perhaps the young of other species). Whilst some responses may be generally accepted (e.g. 'a person who needs the protection of adults'), others might give rise to considerable debate in group or plenary discussion (e.g. 'a person who goes to school' or 'a person under 16'). As their knowledge of childhood and childrearing practices in other societies grows, groups will find it increasingly difficult to arrive at universal definitions.

What is a (British) child? offers a context for students to explore the reality of national character. Was it possible to distil the essential characteristics of, say, a British child as different from a French child or an Indian child? Are there some general characteristics which hold true for a *majority* of children (e.g. place of birth or residence)? What exceptions come to mind? Is it possible to say that British children are different from French or Indian children? Are British children more like Indian children than like British adults?

Who am I? is the most challenging question of all. Why is it so difficult to list those characteristics which mark us out as individuals? Do we, in fact, possess unique characteristics as individuals or is it that our individuality arises from a unique combination of characteristics, none of which obtain to us alone? To what extent would our 'Who am I?' list change from day to day, or during the transition from child to adult?

After the three stages, students can try to analyse the universal, national and individual processes and experiences that make up a child. Further discussion could focus on the degree to which personality characteristics are inherited or acquired.

Source   Based on an activity in D. Wolsk, *An Experience-centered Curriculum*, Educational Studies and Documents No. 17. Paris: UNESCO, 1974.

ACTIVITY 5
Perceptions of beauty

Time needed   40 minutes.

Resources   A set of assorted pictures of young men and women (culled from magazines) for each group of four students; a copy of **Thin is also beautiful** (see p. 21) for each student.

Procedure   *Stage 1*
In mixed-gender groups of four, students are given a random selection of magazine pictures of young men and women. The pictures should encompass a variety of physical characteristics, dress styles and ethnic origins. Each group tries to agree upon the three pictures which represent the 'most beautiful or attractive' men and/or women. Two groups then join to form a larger group of eight, the task now being to attempt agreement on the three most beautiful/attractive men or women from the six pictures available. Where unanimous agreement is not obtainable, a majority verdict will suffice. Once agreement is reached, students are asked to reflect upon and write down the criteria they have used in assessing beauty/attractiveness.

Stage 2
The extract **Thin is also beautiful**, featuring an unnamed girl from the Cook Islands in the South Pacific, is handed out. After reading it, students compile, in their groups of four, a list of all the strategies and ploys they themselves use in an attempt to make themselves look more beautiful or attractive. They then compare this list with the criteria arrived at in Stage 1 to see what relationship exists between the two.

Potential   An activity which helps students explore how culture shapes perceptions of beauty and the extent to which they individually are conditioned by such perceptions. Follow-up discussion could focus on the advantages and disadvantages of conforming/not conforming to the accepted ideals of beauty in our society. Is beauty totally culturally determined or is it partly in the eye of the beholder? Are there some universally accepted notions of beauty? How does age, gender and ethnicity affect individual perceptions of beauty? What is the relationship between physical appearance and self-esteem in young people?

To what extent are words such as 'beautiful' and 'attractive' loaded in terms of gender? How would student reactions have differed if other criteria, such as 'handsome', 'pretty' or 'good-looking', had been used?

Thin is also beautiful

Being plump is considered by my society as the ideal standard of beauty, the symbol of attractiveness and health. To be on the thin side is regarded as inappropriate, and not matching up to society's expectation. Thus as a child and right through to the age of twenty-one, I regarded my thinness as a curse.

Moreover, the fact that I wasn't plump like the rest of the girls my age was of great concern to my parents. Mum would cook all sorts of food just to make me eat, and on top of this I was given a tablespoon of cod-liver oil with an iron tablet every morning. I loathed those doses after breakfast but more often I was told: 'Be a good girl and swallow it, if you want to be fat and beautiful.' The desire to be beautiful, accepted and loved by my parents forced me to go through that every morning.

Every day while dressing for school, I used to stand in front of the mirror to see if I had gained any weight. On the way, I'd stop at the nearest shop and weigh myself. But every time I was disappointed. At school I faced all sorts of names such as 'bony', 'stick' and 'skinny'. Therefore to avoid being ridiculed, I buried myself in my work and kept away from the other children. Many times I desperately wanted to play basketball and tennis but the thought of being laughed at held me back. So I slowly became an isolate.

A year later, I was admitted to a secondary school, and I thought everything would be different. But I was mistaken. The second week I was there, the names were flung at me again. It was at this stage that I decided to try to gain some weight, and every cent I saved was spent on sweets, biscuits and chocolates. On top of this, I ate whatever was laid in front of me. But because I walked to school which was about three miles away from home, I never managed to put on an ounce. I simply noticed that my legs were getting longer than ever. At the age of fourteen I was 5 foot 8 inches and weighed only eight stone. Moreover I earned a new name – *kuea roroa* (long legs).

My height combined with my thinness disturbed me a lot. I yearned for the softness and curves that I saw in other girls, I even dreamed of it and prayed that God would help me gain some weight.

I blamed God for creating me with long legs, long arms and a thin body. Over the years when my dream didn't come true, and my prayers were not answered, I decided to play a different tune altogether.

When they called me 'bony' I laughed in their faces and told them I liked the name. I pretended the names didn't hurt. I also joined the games and the netball team at school, because I knew that isolation wouldn't solve my problems. After the first few weeks in netball, my height became an advantage, and I seemed to be getting all the goals. The others noticed this and started to appreciate me, and I started to develop some pride in my height. Moreover, as most of them couldn't run because of their weight, I again had an advantage over them. This led me to like netball.

I also decided to join the dance team, and here I found that I looked better in a hula skirt than the rest of them. They started to comment how nice I looked in my skirt. As for them, I could see their bulges, and I had no hesitation in pointing it out to them! Perhaps the knowledge that I looked better in a hula skirt made me a better dancer than the rest of them. After a while I noticed that they hated being seen in one. But as dancing is our culture, they had to dance.

During the performance, the thin girl really stood out well. And I ended up being the leader of the team.

Thus although plumpness is still considered by my society as beauty, I have learned to accept my own physique and furthermore proved to my age mates that there are advantages also in being thin!

Source: M. Horsley, 'A life profile to coming of age in the Pacific'. In R. A. C. Stewart (ed.) *Pacific Profiles*. University of the South Pacific, 1982.

ACTIVITY 6
Key events in my life

Time needed	40 minutes.
Resources	Five slips of paper for each student; a **Key events in my life** (p. 23) record sheet for each group of four.
Procedure	Working on their own, students reflect on key events, personal to global, which they feel have had a major influence in shaping their identity, their sense of worth or their relationships with others. They select the five most significant events and write them down, in summary form, on the slips of paper (one on each slip). An 'event' can be interpreted as a one-off occurrence or a longer trend or development. In pairs, students talk about the events and their significance. Two pairs then join and pool their twenty slips of paper. After discarding any slips which duplicate or are very similar in nature to another, the events are written on the **Key events in my life** record sheet and the appropriate box(es) ticked for each one. In considering which boxes to tick students should bear in mind:

– the emphasis is on *could* happen, rather than has happened or will definitely happen;

– it may be appropriate to tick more than one box (e.g. an event which pertains only within one religious group *and* only to girls *and* in many countries);

– very personal events which take place within one's own family or school may well have counterparts in other children's lives (e.g. a special birthday outing; a close relationship with a particular teacher).

The final column is left blank for students to fill in any other relevant heading.

Potential	This activity provides a framework for students to reflect upon those significant events which have shaped their lives and then to postulate on the degree to which such events could also be part of other children's experience. After group reports on the number and nature of events entered in each column, class discussion could focus on the nature of events which are thought to be exclusive to a particular group of people, as contrasted with the type of experiences considered to be more common or universal. Is it important for children to feel that some events are exclusive to their particular group or gender? What is the impact of realizing that many experiences are shared by children throughout the world?

KEY EVENTS IN MY LIFE

A similar event could happen:

EVENT	ONLY WITHIN MY FAMILY	ONLY WITHIN MY SCHOOL/ COMMUNITY	ONLY WITHIN MY SOCIAL/RELIGIOUS /CULTURAL GROUP	ONLY WITHIN MY COUNTRY	ONLY TO CHILDREN OF MY GENDER	TO CHILDREN IN MANY COUNTRIES	TO CHILDREN EVERYWHERE	
1								
2								
3								
4								
5								
6								
7								
8								
9								
10								
11								
12								
13								
14								
15								
16								
17								
18								
19								
20								

ACTIVITY 7
When is an adult?

Time needed	40 minutes.
Resources	One copy of **When is an adult?** chart (p. 25) and one sheet of plain A4 paper for each pair of students.
Procedure	*Stage 1*

Procedure

Stage 1
Working in pairs of the same gender, students draw a time-line on the plain paper:

CHILD ———————————————————— ADULT

Through discussion they decide upon the key steps in the transition from child to adult status and mark them on the line at appropriate points chronologically. After each entry they write in brackets the minimum legal age at which they think a person in the UK may undertake this step; (NL) signifies that they believe there is no law governing this aspect. Finally, they mark with a perpendicular line the point in the transition which they feel is the *watershed* between childhood and adulthood.

Stage 2
Pairs join to form, where possible, a mixed gender group of four. They compare the two time-lines, noting and discussing any significant differences. Groups then report back on their discussions.

Stage 3
Copies of the **When is an adult?** chart are handed out and used as the basis of a class discussion. Is it likely that time-lines marking the transition from child to adult would be similar or very different in other countries indicated on the chart? Would other young people in our own society draw different time-lines? Is there always a relationship between a minimum legal age and what actually happens in practice? Are such laws necessary and, if so, are they always enforceable? What are the social and political implications for countries in which laws vary from one state to another?

Potential

An activity which encourages students to reflect upon the transition from childhood to adulthood and to see this in a global context. Follow-up discussion could explore any differences in perception of the transition between male and female students and the ensuing social ramifications. Was there agreement on the point identified as the watershed and is this related to a particular event, such as leaving school or home? Viewed from an historical perspective, 'coming of age' has, in most societies, fallen from 21 to 18. Is this trend likely to continue and, if so, what are the implications for individuals and societies? For an additional perspective, students could read and discuss the articles on the traditional initiation of Aboriginal boys into manhood, **Initiation** (p. 2) and the ritual ceremony undergone by all girls in Kiribati, **The anointed one** (p. 26).

WHEN IS AN ADULT?

The minimum age when an individual may:	Argentina	Australia	Brazil	Costa Rica	India	Italy	Japan	Kenya	Sweden	Turkey	UK
1 Drive a car	18	VS	18	18	18	18	18	18	18	18	17
2 Vote	18	18	16 - optional 18 - compulsory	18	18	18	20	18	18	19	18
3 Marry (without parental consent)	female 14 male 16	18	18	18	female 18 male 21	18	20	21	18	18	18
4 Drink alcohol	18	18	18	18	18	18	20	18	20	No limit	16
5 Complete compulsory schooling	14	VS	NL	16	16	14	16	NL	16	No limit	16
6 Undertake full-time employment	18	VS	14	18	18 for government service	18	15	18	16	No limit	16
7 Be conscripted	18	No conscription	18	No military forces	No conscription	19	No conscription	NL	18	18	No conscription
8 Leave home	-	VS	-	-	-	18	NL	18	18	18	18
9 Stand for parliament	25 30 Senator	18	21	21	25	25	25 30 for House of Councillors	-	18	30	21

Notes: VS = varies in different states

NL = no legislation

P

The anointed one

As a young girl, I didn't realize how significant it is when a girl reaches a stage of having her first period. I was to learn, however, when a friend of mine began to menstruate. I was surprised when, for quite a few days, I had not seen my friend around. Then someone told me why, so I decided to go and visit her. To my disappointment, I was only allowed to watch from outside the house.

I saw her sitting clad only in a grass skirt, her skin shining with oil. No-one was allowed to talk to her. She, too, was not allowed to speak or to walk about. She had to sit down and work at making string. I hardly saw her eating or drinking and could see that a white palm-tree leaf was tied around her waist. She sat facing the south and her only companion was her grandmother who was carrying out the ritual. I found out that she was not allowed to eat anything beside a piece of dried coconut, with water to drink. She bathed only once a day, when the sun was just setting, and sat from early morning before the sunrise until the afternoon. The water she bathed with was especially prepared by the grandmother, and from what I saw, there were leaves and signs of oil being put in the tub, turning the water to a greenish colour.

This went on for three days, but on the third day, it was different. This time, a lot of her relatives came, because a feast was to be held. She could now speak, but not too much, and was still not allowed to walk about. A special new mat was brought out and she sat on it. Now, she faced a young boy, whom I noticed was the first-born child of the girl's relative. Outside the house, the ground was dug very deep and all the local foods that could be found were cooked in there. This ground oven was to be hers, and no-one was allowed to eat from it before she had taken her food. On the same day, she took a bath and was dressed in a reddish coloured dress. Her skin was oiled.

On her fourth day, she was dressed in another new dress and was now allowed to go out. Most of the relatives had gone back to their homes. I had always been keeping an eye on her, and when she was on her way to fetch some water from the well, I ran to her. I begged her to tell what was the purpose of all those things she was doing. I found out from her that sitting facing south would indicate that her future husband would be from the southern islands, the coconut leaf around her waist would prevent her from getting hungry too easily. The fact that on her third day, she sat facing the first-born child would indicate that she herself would marry a first-born child. She was not allowed to speak because she might spoil the ritual. She ate very little, I noticed, and she said that this would contribute to the idea of not getting hungry too easily. She finished her story and I found myself smiling because I was imagining what would happen if it was done to me. I doubted if I would survive with so little food and drinking water.

Later, I asked my mother why it was so important when a young girl has her first period, that such rituals and a feast have to be held. Her answer to me was that it is the way our society marks the onset of womanhood.

Source: M. Horsley, 'A life profile to coming of age in the Pacific'. In R. A. C. Stewart (ed.) *Pacific Profiles*. University of the South Pacific, 1982.

ACTIVITY 8
Parent power

Time needed	80 minutes.
Resources	A copy of the chart on p. 29 for each student.
Procedure	Working on their own, students complete the chart by imagining how they would react as parents to the situations given. They write a number in each box according to the type of action they would take (the 'Rank' columns to the right should be ignored at this stage).
	Students then form pairs to compare and discuss their individual responses; where they have marked a 5 they should explain what action they would take in this situation. Working as a pair, students now mark the ten situations in order of 'seriousness' at each age level (1 = most serious, 10 = least serious), putting a number in the appropriate box under the 'Rank' columns on the sheet. The facilitator should avoid giving any interpretation of the term 'serious'. Finally, three pairs join together to see if, through discussion and negotiation, they can reach consensus on the ranking at each age level.
Potential	An activity which, in its many stages, provides a framework for students to explore and share their ideas and values on child-rearing and to experiment with different ways of imposing authority and discipline. The potential for further discussion at any stage is enormous, but some of the critical issues are likely to be: How were your opinions on childrearing formed? Have views on what is appropriate/inappropriate behaviour changed since your parents were children? Why is certain behaviour acceptable in some societies but taboo in others (sexual experimentation among children, for example, is encouraged in some societies and, indeed, was commonplace in medieval England)? Was the gender of the imagined child a factor in deciding on the appropriate action? In situation no. 9 (engaging in sexual activity), did you imagine the 'friend' to be of the opposite sex to your 'child'? If so, would your response be different in the case of an envisaged homosexual relationship?
Extension	After the paired discussion of their individual responses, students choose a situation for role play: the 'parent' begins by acting out the path of action previously selected, the 'child' responds to this in the way she thinks appropriate for the age level given. Students could then experiment with different paths of action for the same situation, before changing roles and choosing another situation.
Follow-up	(i) Students read, or have read to them, the extract from 'Childhood in an Indian village' by Wilfred Pelletier. In pairs they try to think of examples of story-telling used in their own upbringing (e.g. good/bad luck superstitions, or phrases such as

'Don't pull that face, it'll stick when the wind changes'). This could be followed by re-examining one of the situations on the chart and devising a suitable story which would put across the appropriate parental message. Stories are then shared with the rest of the class.

(ii) Using similar charts as on p. 29, students ask both parents and grandparents to complete the charts in the following way: (a) how they would respond now (put answers in the first columns); (b) how they would have answered when their children were aged 8–16 (answers in second set of columns). This research task will provide some useful evidence as to how the disciplining of children has changed over recent generations.

And part of the reason our parents say so little is that that's their way. They don't teach like white people; they let their children make their own decisions. The closest they ever got to formal teaching was to tell us stories. Let me give you an example. We had been out picking blueberries one time, and while sitting around this guy told us this story. The idea was that he wanted to get us to wash up – to wash our feet because we had been tramping through this brush all day long. He talked about a warrior who really had a beautiful body. He was very well built, and he used to grease himself and take care of his body. One day this warrior was out, and he ran into a group of other people whom he had never seen before. They started to chase him. He had no problem because he was in such good shape. He was fooling around and playing with them because he was such a good runner. He ran over hills and over rocks, teasing them. Then he ran into another group. The first group gave up the chase. But now he had to run away from this other group, and he was fooling around doing the same thing with them. All of a sudden he ran into a third group. He ran real hard and all of a sudden he fell. He tried to get up and he couldn't. He spoke to his feet and said, 'What's wrong with you? I'm going to get killed if you don't get up and get going.' 'They said, 'That's right. You can comb your hair and grease your body and look after your legs and arms but you never did anything for us. You never washed us or cleaned us or greased us or nothing.' He promised to take better care of the feet if they would get up and run, and so they did.

This is one of the stories we were told, and we went up and washed our feet right away and then went to bed.

Wilfred Pelletier, 'Childhood in an Indian village'. In D. Jay (ed.),
The American Indian: The First Victim. New York: William Morrow, 1972.

If you were a parent and your child aged:	Action			Rank		
	8	12	16	8	12	16
1. wouldn't wear appropriate clothes						
2. drank alcohol at a friend's house						
3. began fighting with a younger child						
4. made an abusive remark about someone of a different racial background						
5. refused to practise their musical instrument						
6. took part in a political demonstration						
7. swore at a relative						
8. smoked a cigarette at home						
9. engaged in sexual activity with a friend of the same age						
10. refused to go to school						

Action possibilities   (enter appropriate number in box)

1. Immediate discipline (e.g. tell off, smack, withdrawal of privilege or pocket money, send to bedroom)

2. Threat (e.g. 'If you do that again, I'll . . .')

3. Reason/explanation (e.g. explain why it was wrong, ask for child's explanation, have a reasoned discussion)

4. No action

5. Other action

ACTIVITY 9
Wit and wisdom

Time needed	One hour.
Resources	A set of badges (at least one per student) inscribed with the proverbs on p. 31. A sheet of chart paper and two felt-tip pens of different colours for each group of four students.
Procedure	*Stage 1*

Working in groups of four, students brainstorm as many proverbs as they can think of, writing them on chart paper with one of the felt-tip pens. They then discuss the basic value(s) or moral(s) which the proverbs underpin and write these next to each proverb, using the second felt-tip pen, e.g.

Proverb	Value(s)/moral(s)
Don't cry over spilt milk	Be practical; don't worry unnecessarily over things you can't change
Too many cooks spoil the broth	Don't interfere in others' affairs
A stitch in time saves nine	Think ahead

Plenary discussion follows, focusing on the use and impact of proverbs in the students' childhood and upbringing.

Stage 2
Students individually select, or are given, a badge to wear. After initial reflection on the meaning of their own proverb, they try to form pairs or groups of people whose proverbs have the same or similar underlying values/morals. Any remaining individuals should be encouraged to join the most appropriate pair/group. After discussing the various proverbs, each pair/group selects one as the basis for a short dramatic sketch which aptly conveys its underlying message. The sketches are presented to the rest of the students, who have to guess what the proverb might be. Plenary discussion follows.

Potential	A light-hearted exploration of the function and signigicance of proverbs in the student's own and other cultures. Discussion could include an analysis of the similarities/differences between proverbs – and their underlying meanings – in various cultures, matching proverbs from other cultures with those derived from Stage 1; an assessment of the appropriateness of selected proverbs as suitable moral guidelines for the late twentieth century (including the language used).
Follow-up	Many opportunities exist for further creative work. Students can illustrate the meanings of selected proverbs through creative writing (e.g. turning the proverb into a fable), or in cartoon form. They can also try to invent new proverbs which portray values that are significant in the late twentieth century, e.g.

- encourage people to embrace new information technology;
- encourage boys to be gentle and caring/girls to be assertive;
- warn of the dangers of environmental destruction;
- warn of the dangers of nationalism/sectarianism.

Source	Centre for Global Education.

Nobody cries who has not been pinched. *Kenya*

An old crow does not croak for nothing. *Russia*

You cannot hold on to two cows at the same time. *Burkina Faso*

A man cannot whistle and drink at the same time. *Denmark*

Do not hold a leopard's tail, but if you hold it, don't let go. *Ethiopia*

If you have to kill a snake, kill it once and for all. *Japan*

He who is starving hates him who is eating. *Gabon*

When one eats and others look on, there is likely to be a fight. *Turkey*

In multitude there is strength. *Nigeria*

United we stand, divided we fall. *United States*

A bad brother is far better than no brother. *Swahili – East Africa*

Blood is thicker than water. *Norway*

The wise child is spoken to in proverbs, not in simple language. *Ghana*

The wise child listens to his elders. *Italy*

Unless you fill up the crack, you will have to build a new wall. *Ewe – West Africa*

A stitch in time saves nine. *Holland*

Fair speech turns elephants away from the garden path. *Swahili – East Africa*

Gentle words open iron gates. *Bulgaria*

Time passes on but sayings remain. *India/Sri Lanka*

Learn proverbs well and good speech will come naturally. *China*

A rotten tree does not produce fruits, and empty words have no value. *China*

Together, people can move mountains; firewood bunched together can produce higher flames. *China*

Pain in the finger affects the whole body. *Philippines*

One who does not know how to dance blames the flooring. *Burma*

A pumpkin thief is known by his shoulder. *Sri Lanka*

The hardest rock erodes in water. *Philippines*

Repairing the cow-shed after the cow is lost. *Rep. of Korea*

A sparrow does not skim over a rice mill. *Rep. of Korea*

Constant grinding can turn even iron into a needle. *China*

Where elephants fight, the seeds get hurt. *Tanzania*

Unity among the small makes the lion lie down hungry. *Swahili – East Africa*

By trying often, the monkey learns to jump from the tree. *Congo*

We must all hang together or we'll all hang separately. *United States*

Better slip of the foot than of the tongue. *France*

He who looks not before, finds himself behind. *France*

Begin in time to finish without hurrying. *Germany*

He conquers who sticks in the saddle. *Italy*

Where there are too many cooks the soup will be salt. *Italy*

Truth and oil always come to the surface. *Spain*

The wise man does not hang his knowledge on a hook. *Spain*

ACTIVITY 10
Games children play

Time needed	40 minutes.
Resources	A copy of a **Games children play** chart (p. 33) for each group of four students.
Procedure	Working in groups of four, students list the games that they have played as children with an emphasis on those games which were initiated and conducted by children, rather than led or supervised by adults. Both indoor and outdoor games should be included. From the lists so compiled, the ten games most commonly played – as identified by each group – are entered on the **Games children play** chart. Through discussion, groups complete – by ticking the appropriate boxes – the remaining three sections of the chart: who generally plays the game (boys, girls or both); what skills are *principally* practised; what underlying values and attitudes are fostered, intentionally or otherwise. Students can insert additional skills and values/attitudes in the blank columns. Class discussion follows, perhaps beginning by ascertaining the skills and values/attitudes most and least ticked by each group. A comparison between the skills and values/attitudes associated with 'boys only' and 'girls only' games could initiate reflection and discussion on how games contribute to the socialization into and formation of gender roles and the reinforcement of stereotypes. Discussion might also focus on the ratio of co-operative to competitive games, the reasons for this and some wider implications.
Potential	An activity which stimulates thinking about the function of games in the socialization of children and the extent to which 'playing' develops significant skills and attitudes.
Follow-up	Students compile a checklist – based on the **Games children play** chart – to aid their observation of girls' and boys' play in a local infant or junior school. The research data are collated back in class and discussion ensues.

33

		1	2	3	4	5	6	7	8	9	10	11	12	13	14	15	16	17	18	19	20
VALUES AND ATTITUDES																					
	Exclusion of others																				
	Tolerance of others																				
	National/cultural identity																				
	Personal advancement																				
	Establishing superiority																				
	Self-esteem building																				
	Competition																				
	Co-operation																				
SKILLS																					
	Imagination																				
	Intellect/logic																				
	Concentration																				
	Patience/persistence																				
	Assertiveness																				
	Teamwork																				
	Agility/dexterity																				
	Speed																				
	Strength																				
PLAYED BY	Both																				
	Girls only																				
	Boys only																				
GAME																					

ACTIVITY 11
My world, my future

Time needed   Two hours, or a few lessons.

Resources   Writing paper and copies of **My world in the year 2000**.

Procedure   *Stage 1*

Each student is asked to write, anonymously, a short essay (*c.* 500 words) entitled 'My world in 21 years' time'. On completion, the essays are collected in and randomly redistributed around the class so that no student has her own essay. Students are now asked to analyse the essays according to the following criteria:

(a) to what extent is the student's vision of the future optimistic and/or pessimistic?

(b) to what extent is the future vision realistic and/or unrealistic?

(c) to what extent is the future vision personally oriented and/or globally oriented?

Working now in groups of six, students share their analyses and compile a group report which represents a collective analysis of their six essays. A plenary reporting and discussion stage follows, the aim of which is to establish the range of visions that exist and to encourage students to reflect upon the origins of their visions.

Stage 2

Copies of **My world in the year 2000** are handed out and it is explained that these essays or extracts were written in 1979. Returning to their former groups of six, students discuss the readings in terms of the criteria used previously, with a particular emphasis on assessing the extent to which they now think the visions are realistic or unrealistic. Class discussion follows. Finally, in the light of the ideas and thoughts generated throughout the activity, students write a brief commentary on the essays they originally analysed and hand them back to the authors.

Potential   This is a thought-provoking activity designed to raise students' awareness of their perceptions of the future and the extent to which these are universally shared or culturally conditioned. Some of the key questions for consideration and discussion are: How does an individual's future vision develop? To what extent does it direct or influence present practice? Do factors such as gender and social class have any significant bearing on future perspectives? Can there be future visions that are universally shared? To what extent are optimism and pessimism regarding the future derived from a similar view of oneself and one's contribution to society? How can individuals help turn their preferred future into reality?

My World in the Year 2000
It would be nice to have something that wouldn't change

The year 2000 is too much a radical change for me to think about. But it's one of the reasons that I want to move out of this country. I'm kind of getting future shock here. It scares me that so much is happening at once, like moving house a lot, losing old friends and new friends being rushed on me too fast. It would be nice if I could have something to latch onto that wouldn't change or run away from me.

I'll try to think about a day in Year 2000 for the normal person. He'll get up in the morning and turn on the tri-tube (three-dimensional television) and quickly get all the news that is happening today – the wars, how many people are getting killed in Lebanon and so on – for about 10 minutes. Then he goes down the bounce tube which is like an elevator except it works by anti-gravity. He gets into his air-pressured car and shoots to work at 150 miles an hour watching some more of the tri-tube. He presses a few buttons and does paper-work and then goes home to his wife and kids.

In the evening he won't be able to go out because it's not safe and there is a curfew at 8.00. Every night he hears about 20 screams and 10 gunshots. So in the evening he plays computer games and watches the tri-tube. Television phones will be very popular then. Houses will be about the same as now. I think they are still going to have rugs, transparent nylon shiny rugs where you can see the floor underneath like the ones you see in commercials for floor wax.

On the weekend the man goes out to a pleasure farm where they have real trees (not the plastic kind) and water that you can swim in without wearing protective suits. He can't do this too often because there is a constant line of people who want his job so he has to be pretty good at it or he is out.

It would not be like that for me. I am getting out. I am going to be a vet. Not the kind that takes care of French poodles. I am going to Africa. They need vets there.

I want my wife to work with me. It would be more income into the house. I don't want to be poor but I don't want to be super-snobbish rich either.

When the kids are really young my wife's probably going to take a few years off. I'd like to take off just as much time as she to take care of the kids because that is what a father should do.

I might want to marry either a widow or a divorcee who already has a kid, because I don't relish the thought of raising a little child for two or three years. I want to have a child about the age where I can make an impression on him. He will learn my ideas and appreciate them and maybe think them over and use them.

I'd have very high ambitions for my kids. I want my kids to be professional people – medicine or law – I don't want them to be plumbers or labourers or anything like that. I kind of want them to be better than me. My father was a Rhodes scholar and went to schools on scholarships. My mother won lots of scholarships too. That kind of upsets me, because I am never going to be like that.

John Paden, 14, Illinois, USA
Source: *New Internationalist* **76**, June 1979

My World in the Year 2000
I am a Bangladeshi to every cell of my body

In the Year 2000 I would be 38. There is every possibility that I may not be still alive. But if I am, I will be an architect. I want to build buildings which will not only beautify the world but bring happiness. People who live in my buildings cannot help but smile and be happy.

I will live in Bangladesh because I am a Bangladeshi to every cell of my body. So I have spiritual relations with the soil, water and soul of every other Bangladeshi. And for this reason I intend to live in Bangladesh as long as I live.

Bangladesh wants many things from me. The responsibility to develop this country will be our responsibility.

Most of the people of our country are cultivators. They work hard, heart and soul. But the tools for cultivation are poor. In the Year 2000 there will be better tools and with hard work there will be more food. The poor people will not die from famine and our country will be developed like America, Japan, Russia and China. Then we will all live happily.

The houses by then will not be made of mud. They will be stone and will not fall down easily. Bridges will be made over the rivers and good roads will run from town to town. Everything will be changed except for our favourite rice and fish.

There will be machines. But the machines should not take the vitality out of you and take out the happiness evident in small things. There should be pitchforks for pitching hay, for example, but I would like a machine to wake me up and give me tea in the morning.

Population growth threatens the nation. By 2000 AD the population will be nearly doubled and it will be impossible to live in Bangladesh. If all of us only have two children then it will be possible to live in this land. I will only have two children. I know that if I marry I will never be able to shine in my life, but even then I dream of having children.

When my own parents are old I will of course want them to stay with me. Then I will be able to make sure that they are happy and comfortable and it will be my chance to love them though I can never give back the love they have given me all their lives.

Finally I aspire that in the Year 2000 AD there will be one nation, and that is human beings; that there is one race and that is the human race; and that there is one religion and that is humanity; and that there is one country and that is the earth; and lastly that the entire mankind may lead a harmonious life of peaceful existence and tolerance.

Anawara Khan, 15, Dacca, Bangladesh

The endless rows of trees will be gone and there will be barbed wire instead. Really, I don't think there'll be anything after the Year 2000. I just think it will stop then.

Bjorn Kellman, 15, Sweden

Source: *New Internationalist* **76**, June 1979

My World in the Year 2000

In 2000 AD I will be a farmer. I will have a dip and fences for my cattle. I will have crop rotation and fertilisers. I hope to do a lot for the country so everyone will have a lot of food.

Tom Odhiambo, 14, Kenya

I don't ever want to go broke. The husband I have would have to be in pretty good shape moneywise because of the lifestyle I've grown up with. I want the same level of living because it's hard to drop down.

Tracy Cernan, 15, USA

I don't want to be rich. People just envy you. Why should you have more than you need? Once you've got a home, family, friends and a job you should be satisfied.

Desmond Thomas, 14, Jamaica

My feather alarm tickles my feet. I get up and my robot, Gaston, serves breakfast. Electronic life is OK but boring. I take my helicopter to work and check that the orders I gave yesterday are obeyed.

Valerie Bouget, 14, France

The houses will be made of stone. They will cost $250 and will last a long time. The roads will be made of tar. There will not be any beggars and poor people. Everyone will have jobs and food.

Asanatu Koroma, 13, Sierra Leone

I picture myself coming home at, say, six o'clock. I've been away acting in a play on Broadway. I kiss my wife – maybe she won't be my wife. We have a middle-class house with rounded corners.

David Wall, 12, Canada

In the Year 2000 I want there to be peace and I want all parents to be like mine, to understand their children and not beat them. Some parents beat them on the head with wire which can damage their eyes.

Maribel Olaya, 11, Peru

When we are adults the United Nations will be even stronger. Then it will order all countries to get rid of weapons which can extinguish life on earth. Most countries have not yet realized the importance of the UN.

Kariuki Kihiko, 15, Kenya

We will stop industry, which keeps going deeper and deeper into nature, and save from extinction all rare species and help animals to live in the wilderness.

Danuta Adamczyk, 14, Poland

Source: *New Internationalist* **76**, June 1979

ACTIVITY 12
A class convention on the rights of the child

Time needed   3 hours (can be spread over several lessons).

Resources   180 white cards made by cutting A4 sheets into quarters, 30 cards of another colour, about 22 sheets of chart paper, six felt-tip pens, 30 copies of the **Summary of the Convention on the Rights of the Child** sheet (pp. 6–7).

Procedure   It is explained to the class that an international Convention (agreement) on the Rights of the Child was adopted by the UN General Assembly in November 1989. The idea of the Convention is to provide an effective protection for children by laying down a universally agreed and detailed statement of their rights. The Convention identifies, for the first time, a comprehensive and discrete rights agenda for children. States signing it commit themselves to providing special safeguards for children's rights over and above the protection afforded to all citizens. The Convention, which has 54 clauses and lays down some 35 rights, needed to be ratified by at least 20 countries before it could come into force and, hence, bind signatory nations. The twentieth country ratified the Convention on 3 August 1990 and it came into effect one month later on 2 September 1990. By September 1997, 191 countries had ratified the Convention. Students are informed that their task is to forge their own Convention on the Rights of the Child.

Each student is given six white cards and one coloured card and is asked to write down six rights children should have (one right per white card). On the coloured card students are asked to write down their definition of what childhood is and at what ages they think it begins and ends (i.e. the period during which the individual should enjoy the special protection of a Convention on children's rights). Discussion should be avoided whilst the cards are being written.

Students then form groups of five with the task of drawing up a first draft of their Convention. The first stage is to read through the group's 36 white cards and to arrange them in clusters on the floor or table area where they are working. Clusters are to be made up of cards describing similar types of rights. A cluster may be one card describing a particularly distinctive right.

The group now compiles its list of children's rights. The list should contain between ten and fifteen items. This may mean that the group will have to omit certain ideas entirely, collapse cards in the same cluster together or simply edit two or more closely approximating cards so they stand as one rights statement. The group must decide upon an appropriate ordering of rights (the clusters will help here). Their other task is to agree on a preamble to their list explaining what childhood is and identifying when it begins and ends (the six coloured cards should be used as a springboard for discussion). The group's draft convention, i.e. preamble followed by list of rights, is written up on one or two sheets of chart paper.

Groups are next asked to join with another group and to negotiate and write down on chart paper an agreed second draft of the Convention, using their respective first drafts as a starting point for discussion. The second draft should contain an agreed preamble and a list of no more than twenty rights. The combined groups then present their second drafts in plenary session. Class discussion follows around the merits and demerits of each draft, the eventual aim being to secure agreement on and write down a class Convention on the Rights of the Child containing an agreed preamble and no more than 35 rights (further chart paper should be available). The resulting Convention is posted on the classroom wall.

Students then return to their combined groups of ten, each with a summary of the UN Convention on the Rights of the Child. They are asked to compare and contrast it with their own work (the preamble and list of rights). Are there any important children's rights the class had overlooked? Why were they overlooked? Could the UN Convention be strengthened by including items from the class's list? In what ways would the group like to amend the class Convention having read the UN Convention?

Students are once again brought together in plenary session to discuss their responses to the UN Convention and to propose amendments to their own work (these can be voted upon). Discussion follows.

Potential

This sequence of activities offers a student-centred introduction to the UN Convention on the Rights of the Child. Typically, it will take students through a process of challenge in which they are increasingly confronted by different perspectives on what children's rights should embrace. As they move from working in small to combined groups and from combined groups to the class group, they will find that others have thought of rights that never occurred to them. The limitations of their perspective will be brought into sharpest focus when introduced to the UN Convention. There is often a sense of shock here as students realize that they have overlooked, or taken for granted, rights of a fundamental nature or rights of central importance to particular groups of children. The ethnocentrism of class perspectives should be fully teased out in the final plenary.

The chain of discussion triggered off by the coloured cards is intended to simulate the problems faced by the UN Working Group on the draft Convention (representing 43 member states). The group found it very difficult to arrive at an internationally acceptable definition of childhood. There are significantly divergent perceptions from one country to another regarding the age at which childhood ends and the child's economic role in the family and society begins. There are also debates surrounding when childhood begins (is the unborn foetus a 'child'?). The Working Group, therefore, had to face the fundamental question of whether an international set of children's rights was feasible and useful. The coloured cards, and the contents of the preambles, as fashioned in initial groups and as revised in combined groups and class plenary, can be used to confront this same question.

Variations

1. Having arrived at a class Convention on the Rights of the Child, students watch one or more films exploring the lives of children in different parts of the world (see the list of audiovisual materials on p. 90 for titles). After each film they return to their combined groups of ten to reassess the class Convention (including the preamble) in the light of what they have seen. Suggestions for amendment are brought to plenary session, discussed and put to the vote. Students then receive a summary of the actual Convention on the Rights of the Child to stimulate further reflection, discussion and amendment (as described in the last two paragraphs of the *Procedure* section).

2. Students bring to class, or are given, newspaper stories depicting children under threat whether from war or civil disturbance, poverty, environmental degradation or individual/institutional abuse. In their combined groups of ten they assess whether the class Convention (including the preamble) is sufficiently thoroughgoing, rigorous and comprehensive to fully protect the children in the stories. If not, proposals for amendments and additions are brought to plenary session, discussed and voted upon.
The same activity can be used following the introduction of the UN Convention to the class as a means of checking its comprehensiveness.

Follow-up

Students, based on their experiences of this activity, compose a formal letter to the Education Officer of UNICEF (see address on p. 92), outlining what they regard as the strengths and weaknesses of the UN Convention, and enclosing a copy of their class Convention.

ACTIVITY 13
Perspectives on children's rights

Time needed   Two hours, or several lessons.

Resources   180 white cards made by cutting A4 sheets into quarters, ten sheets of chart paper, six felt-tip pens, 36 copies of the **Summary of the Convention on the Rights of the Child** (pp. 6–7), six copies of each of the **identity sheets** (pp. 43–8) used. Blu-tack.

Procedure   The class divides into groups of five to six. Each group member takes, and carefully reads, one of the identity sheets. Taking on the identity of the child described in the sheet the student drafts six rights (one per card) that she thinks the child would particularly want included in an international Convention on the Rights of the Child. This is done without reference to other group members. Then, staying in role, the group members come together to negotiate a Convention. As a first step in the process, they introduce themselves and their situation to others in the group before proceeding to explain their choice of rights. The group then takes the shuffled cards one by one and jointly discusses whether to place them on an 'agree' pile (i.e. from all our perspectives this is an important right and, we are all happy with the way it is expressed) or a 'hold' pile (i.e. 50 per cent or more of us think this is important and, with due amendment, this could be included in the 'agree' pile) or a 'disagree' pile (i.e. less than 50 per cent of us think this is an important right). Attention then turns specifically to the 'hold' pile and the group tries to rework each 'card' to the satisfaction of all members. So reworked, they are placed on the 'agree' pile.

Still in role, group members then draw up their Convention on the Rights of the Child using the 'agree' cards as a basis. The group should agree upon an appropriate ordering and grouping of the cards, collapsing together rights that closely overlap. The Convention is written out on chart paper.

Group Conventions are stuck to the wall and groups go to inspect each other's work. Class discussion follows. In what ways are the finished products different? In what ways are they similar? Having seen the other Conventions, are students happy that their own Convention represented the rights priorities of the child whose identity they assumed as well as it might have done?

At an appropriate point, summaries of the UN Convention of the Rights of the Child are distributed. Groups re-form to compare and contrast the work of the UN with their own work. Their reflections are shared in a further plenary discussion.

Potential   An excellent way of helping students look at children's rights from a range of different perspectives (the discussion of the various group Conventions and of the UN Convention can also be undertaken in role if deemed appropriate).

This activity can be inserted into the sequence of tasks making up Activity 12 – immediately after the class Convention has been drawn up and before the actual UN Convention is introduced. The final debriefing can then focus upon comparing and contrasting the class Convention, the Convention devised 'in role' and the UN Convention.

IDENTITY SHEET 1

Mustafa, India

Mustafa lives in Moradabad, two hours from Delhi. The day I made the journey to Moradabad, it was hot outside: 45 degrees Celsius, 113 degrees Fahrenheit. Where Mustafa works, it was hotter still, well over 50 degrees Celsius, because his job is to attend the roaring furnaces and pour the molten metal into the moulds of the town's brass industry. It is a fascinating process, quite beautiful as the white-hot metal illuminates his face and skin. He is lucky in that his exposed flesh and bare feet have not yet been scarred by drops and shards of hot metal, as so many others have. But Mustafa is only 8 years old, and has only been working here for a year or two; he cannot remember exactly how long.

He has never been to school, nor have any of his workmates. Such high accomplishments as reading, writing and arithmetic are reserved for the wealthier sections of society, like those who employ him. Mustafa does not have much to count. He only gets 3 rupees a day, about 12p, though that does cover his basic need, food. Without his income, he and his brothers would go hungry. His father only makes 200 rupees a month (£8), and there are six mouths to feed. There used to be seven, but Mustafa's little sister died of tuberculosis last year. He was sad about that, but not exactly shattered. In India, you get used to death at an early age. Out of every thousand children 149 die before they reach the age of five; and Moradabad claims the highest incidence of TB in India, a country where the condition is endemic.

The conditions in the brass workshops are the main culprit, though Mustafa's workshop was by no means the worst. It is a relatively large shed, open at one end to the air. In summer, that air is hot, but you are not much aware of it when crouched over the flames of the furnaces, which are sunk beneath the floor. Mustafa and his mates carry the heavy ingots of crude metal, they prime and stoke the under-floor furnaces, they pour the white-hot liquid brass into the moulds, they empty and clean them, they grind and polish the brassware on lathes powered by lethally flailing overhead drive-belts. Sparks and shards of metal fly, accidents occur. Nobody knows how many: no records are kept. But the worst health problems are less easily seen. They are caused by the dust-laden air and the chemicals used in electroplating, by the long hours working huddled in low light levels, and by malnutrition. Mustafa does not often eat a balanced meal, though at least his culture retains the knowledge of how to make the best of limited means. That knowledge did not save his sister from an early grave, or others from the many poverty-related diseases which decimate their ranks. Yet that is the main reason why people continue to have such large families: to provide the family unit with an adequate number of little working hands to fill the pot, despite the high infant mortality.

All population statistics in India are approximate, but they reckon about 40 per cent of this industrious workforce are children.

Source: P. Lee-Wright, *Child Slaves*. London: Earthscan, 1990.

IDENTITY SHEET 2

Frank, USA

Frank is 16 years old. And home for him today is a prison cell. He lives in a top-security wing of a detention centre in New York City, convicted for selling drugs and taking them himself.

Ironically, Frank counts himself one of the lucky ones. It is this prison that has provided him – for the first time in his life – with a stable environment and contact with adults he can trust. These adults have helped him stay on a drug rehabilitation programme and enrol on a study course. Frank wants to be trained as a social worker, to help other children who end up on the streets as addicts or prostitutes after they have been abandoned by their parents.

He knows what being abandoned is like. When he was 13 he was sent away to summer camp. When he came home a few weeks later, he found the house vacant. He searched through the house but his mother's closets no longer contained her clothes. The kitchen had no food in it. His mother and step-father had simply moved out – and left no forwarding address.

'My parents had gone', he says. 'I didn't understand what had happened or why.' He sat shocked and bewildered on the steps, not knowing what to do next until a neighbour took pity on him, and called him in to break the shattering news.

Once he had recovered from his immediate shock, he turned to his biological father for shelter. His father had a large apartment but: 'He said he was renting out all his rooms.'

Parents are supposed to provide a secure base for their children: parents like Frank's provide a foundation of duplicity and rejection. Frank spent the next three years learning how to fend for himself. Sometimes he was taken on by the state authorities who sent him off to one temporary foster home after another. But Frank found himself pushed out again and again. 'They all want to be your parents at first', he says bitterly. 'But they let you go real quick. I must have went through 30 "parents".'

Frank is not alone. Abandoned teenagers taken into state care tend to be bounced from one welfare placement to another – until they give up and return to the street, making a dangerous living by stealing or by selling drugs or their bodies. Those who do not catch AIDS, get pregnant or become addicted to crack and often fall ill with pneumonia or malnutrition, through poor shelter and junk food. Many children are so depressed they attempt suicide.

Many of the rich world's runaways are really 'throwaways' like Frank, scapegoated for family troubles and abandoned. Even the children who have run away are children fleeing profoundly damaging situations at home. As many as half the children who find their way to teenage shelters in New York have been physically or sexually abused at home. Any serious initiatives to counter the problem of children of the street must begin with preventive work within families to stop children being abused at home. Any other answer is like sending an ambulance to the bottom of a cliff.

Source: A. Vittachi, *Stolen Childhood*, North South Productions, 1989.

IDENTITY SHEET 3

Lilian, Australia

At the age of 6, Lilian was taken by a Welfare Officer from her home where she lived with her mother and grandmother. Like many of the tens of thousands of Aboriginal children taken from their families throughout the twentieth century Lilian was not able to contact her mother – nor was her mother ever informed of her whereabouts.

The Welfare Officer had been required to complete a form giving reasons for taking the child, but it was sufficient to write that she was 'neglected' or 'uncontrollable'. The officer genuinely believed that Lilian was better off removed from the poverty of her grandmother's home and placed in an environment where she could be brought up like a white child. However the girls' home to which she was sent at Cootamundra terrified Lilian. Although many of the staff were kind and their material needs were met, there was little affection at the home. Lilian could not visit her home – nor was she allowed to communicate with other Aboriginal families. Much of her spare time after school was spent doing chores – particularly washing and cleaning. The superintendent's obsession with cleanliness reflected her dislike of blackness and her belief that it was in her wards' best interests to marry white men so that their children might pass as 'white'.

Between the ages of 8 and 16 Lilian was fostered by a number of white families – normally childless – who were selected because of their comfortable standard of living and 'moral tone'. Apart from some very happy times Lilian did not enjoy this time of her life. She resisted attempts of one family to impose their religious beliefs upon her. Some of their family only wanted her as a domestic servant – and gave her little freedom to play as she chose. Even in the one family where she felt genuinely loved and respected she missed her own mother and other relatives. As an Aborigine she never really felt accepted in the white community – but was concerned that she didn't really know much about what the Aboriginal community was like.

When, at age 16, she was no longer under the Welfare Department's control she left the family she was living with to try to find her mother and relatives.

Source: based upon data from P. Read, *The Stolen Generations: The Removal of Aboriginal Children in New South Wales, 1883–1969*. Sydney: New South Wales Ministry of Aboriginal Affairs, 1982.

IDENTITY SHEET 4

Janete, Brazil

Life in Novo Hamburgo, in the southern state of Rio Grande do Sul, is dominated by footwear, particularly women's shoes. Apart from supplying the large domestic market, this is an important export industry, with six million pairs a year going to Britain, and many more to the United States. With 30 major factories, and 170 smaller ones, the industry employs over 35,000 people in Novo Hamburgo, at least 12,000 of them being minors. Even in the market leader Sibisa's showpiece factory, which has a modern plant, machinery and work pattern, with an established union organization, I saw many children employed. Janete Rodrigues de Rosa is 14. When I met her, she had been working for Sibisa for fourteen months; before that, she had worked in another factory for two years. Although she is quite tall for her age, she has a pale washed-out look about her – as if she has seen a ghost, but not quite woken. This is a common look in these parts, as we heard when we accompanied Janete to see Dr Rosario Silva at the clinic run by the Sindicato do Calcado, the Shoeworkers' Union.

Janete was just the latest to come in with a disturbing set of symptoms which the good doctor had identified as common among those working with glue in the shoe factories.

'The law prohibits the sale of glue to children, but does nothing to stop them working nine hours a day in an atmosphere laden with these benzine-based solvents. . . . Children are more susceptible than adults to their effects, and should not be working with them . . . There is normally inadequate ventilation, so that the vapour hangs around the work floor. They should never eat in these areas but they do, many bringing packed lunches which sit beside the work-bench for hours absorbing the fumes before the children eat. They should also never smoke in the factory, for the fumes condense in the cigarette smoke as it is inhaled, causing droplets to congeal in the lungs. . . . A lot of children have parents at home who do *atelier* work [outwork], so, after a day working with glue, they go home to a kitchen reeking of it, and ingest more food impregnated with it. There should be legislation against this use of child labour, making it a crime.'

After a year of developing reactions to the glue, Janete asked to be moved to another job, but her employer refused, so she left. She was also keen to continue schooling at evening class, which is supposed to be available to all minors. But the hours they work, and the travel to and from home, make this impossible for most, even if they wish it. She had started one course in a class of 40, but only 12 made it to the end, and only half passed the exam.

Source: P. Lee-Wright, *Child Slaves*. London: Earthscan, 1990.

IDENTITY SHEET 5

Gopamma, India

Gopamma, aged eight, looks immaculate. Not a hair is out of place as it is smoothed back and divided into two crisp braids. Red ribbons match the red of her dress. Gopamma looks out from this neat frame: an intelligent, vulnerable and classically beautiful child. We are charmed even before she comes forward to greet us – and then startled.

For the perfectly groomed child with the perfect face had dropped down on all fours to walk. The small of her back is raised high in the air as she perches on hands and feet, legs stiffly stretched, head down.

Walking even like this is a victory. When Gopamma was two she caught the polio virus from the polluted water in her North Indian village – water that is still used by the villagers today: they have no alternative. After her illness Gopamma couldn't walk at all. She could move only by folding her legs underneath her like a cross and dragging herself slowly forward with her hands – or slithering on her belly 'like a snake', as her father describes it, distressed at the recollection.

Of those sad days, Gopamma says, 'I couldn't go to school and I couldn't play'. The other children ignored her or made fun of her – except for one little girl, Nagalakshmi, who has remained her friend. Most of the day, says Gopamma's mother, the little girl would sit by the side of the road with a sad face, looking at the other children playing. To see the world beyond her home, Gopamma had to hitch a ride on the back of her 10-year-old brother Malleswara, or be carried about like a baby in her father's arms.

But, much as he loved his daughter, her father had little time and energy to spare. The family owns just half an acre of land so, after doing his own farming, Gopamma's father has to hire himself out as a labourer on other people's farms to earn an extra 10 to 15 rupees a day (about US $1) to make ends meet.

Gopamma had her first corrective surgery to straighten and strengthen her legs when she was discovered by the Arthik Samata Mandal, an organization founded on Gandhian principles. They had built a hospital with financial help from The Save the Children Fund. She has had two operations so far; after a third, she should be able to walk upright.

But Gopamma's six years of immobility need never have happened if Gopamma's parents had known about immunizing their children. A few cents' worth of polio vaccine could have prevented Gopamma's paralysis for a minute fraction of the cost of the expensive and painful curative operations.

Now Gopamma can go to school, and is busy catching up on her lost years of education. When she grows up, she says, she is going to become a teacher who spreads the immunization message. Her words are likely to carry extra weight, since she has come to understand the value of immunization by such a hard route.

Source: A. Vittachi, *Stolen Childhood*, North South Productions, 1989.

IDENTITY SHEET 6

Eva and Josie, Philippines

On the face of it Olangapo looks no worse than any other 'Fun City' from Blackpool to Las Vegas. Its 550 night clubs, bars, cheap hotels, sauna baths and massage parlours only go into full swing when the boats come in. Sailors have an average $50 a day each to spend in the few days before their ship sails. It mostly goes on women and drink. Unofficial estimates of numbers involved in prostitution range from 20,000 full-time to 50,000 part-time, with as many as 20,000 children involved.

When I first arrived on these streets of gaudy neon, I was assaulted by the sights and sounds of the bars, as the barkers open the doors to entice you in as you pass, and by the girls themselves, whose exploring hands leave you in no doubt as to their line of business. But the most disturbing characters were the pimps, who favour the less well-lit parts of the street to join you as you walk and engage your interest in their wares. Always high on the list were young girls and 'virgins'. They were asking as little as 150 or 200 pesos (£4.50–£6.00) for sex with a child as young as 10.

Five months later, I returned to find the streets festooned with banners and messages welcoming the arrival in harbour of the Australian Navy's *HMAS Swan*. The girls dancing behind the bars were called down from their platforms, bought drinks and bought out for the night in the time-honoured fashion. The children hung around the periphery, waiting for the deviant interest that paid their way. That is where Eva, who was 13, and her 10-year-old friend Josie hung out. They had both been having commercial sex with foreign servicemen and tourists for three years. A hundred times I have seen the moment on film when Josie admits to starting on the game at the age of 7, and it still catches me on the raw.

Eva: 'We don't like the tourists much, but some help us. They give us money and they give us clothes. But it is all bad – it's all prostitution here.'
Josie: 'I don't know – sometimes it's good. I had my education here.'
Eva: 'When we have nothing to eat at home, then we go with the tourists. Sometimes we go away with them, for a week or a month.'
Josie: 'For a month we get a thousand pesos [£30], or if they are really generous, a thousand a week. But sometimes it's only a hundred [£3].'
Eva: 'We have pimps and they take 80 of every 100 pesos we earn. Then sometimes, when the pimps are caught by the police, the police ask them for the money, or ask the customers.'
Josie: 'Sometimes, when the police have no money, they pick us up for vagrancy. Then they ask us for money so they can go gambling.'
Eva: 'Sometimes we really want to change, but we aren't really able to because we need the money.'

By the age of 13, Eva had the body language of a seasoned streetwalker and the eyes of someone who had seen it all. Josie was 10 and still had the body and behaviour of a primary-school girl. But the depths of her experience showed in her eyes too, reflecting on the things she did to earn money for food. Both sniffed glue, to inure themselves against the daily horror of their reality, but they both needed more to protect them from the marauding foreigner.

Source: P. Lee-Wright, *Child Slaves*. London: Earthscan, 1990.

ACTIVITY 14
Unchaining children

Time needed   One hour fortnightly.

Resources   A stock of strips of paper, 7 cm × 25 cm, copies of the **Summary of the Convention on the Rights of the Child** (pp. 6–7).

Procedure   Working in pairs, students summarize one or two of the rights laid out in the Convention on the Rights of the Child on the paper strip(s) provided, illustrating it/them with an appropriate logo. The strips are then joined in a paper chain hung across the classroom. (The class can discuss which links in the chain would be best next to each other.) The chain should be hung as high as possible to enable further information to be suspended from each link in the chain.

Students then reflect on life at home, at school or elsewhere over the last week and try to remember two things they did for friends or younger children which were in some way beneficial to them. Each action is summarized on a separate strip of paper. The strips are read to the class one by one and the class decides which children's right was supported or enhanced by the action in question. The strip is then hung from the appropriate link in the rights chain. Hence 'I listened to my younger sister read' would be linked to 'every child has the right to an education'.

After all the strips have been hung from the chain, the class discuss which rights they have most supported and which others they were in a position to support, but had failed to do so. Individual students then write messages to themselves on postcards listing three things they intend to do in the next fortnight to advance children's rights. The postcards are placed in a sealed envelope and put in the teacher's safekeeping.

At the end of the fortnight, the postcards are unsealed and returned to enable students to monitor their commitment. The monitoring can be undertaken individually or, in the case of a well-affirmed class, in groups. Students then each write up to two further strips summarizing two of their actions in the past fortnight. These are similarly read out, discussed and hung from the rights chain. If deemed appropriate, further messages to oneself can be written and the process repeated.

Potential   A very enjoyable activity intended to promote a consciousness of rights questions in daily life and a sense of responsibility for advancing and respecting the rights of other children. The activity makes the important point that, whilst it is first and foremost the duty of adults to protect the rights of children, children have responsibilities to each other, too.

Variation   Students are asked to seek out and bring to school articles in the press which have a bearing on children's rights. These are discussed, summarized and hung from the appropriate right in the chain.

Source

After an idea in C. C. Anderson, 'Human rights in elementary and middle schools'. In M. Stimmann Branson and J. Torney-Purta (eds), *International Human Rights, Society, and the Schools*. Washington; DC: National Council for the Social Studies, 1982, p. 54.

ACTIVITY 15
Righting wrongs

Time needed   25 minutes.

Resources   A copy of the **Summary of the Convention on the Rights of the Child** sheet (pp. 6–7) and of one of the **case studies** (pp. 53–9) for each student. A copy of the **Righting wrongs** sheet illustrated below for each group.

Procedure   Students form groups of four (group members should all have the same case study). They read the case study before going on to complete the four columns of the **Righting wrongs** sheet (the **Convention on the Rights of the Child** summary sheets are used as a checklist for completing the first column). In cases where groups have all worked upon the same case study, a column-by-column class debriefing can then follow. Where both case studies have been used, groups can be asked to offer a presentation as a prelude to plenary discussion.

Potential   An activity that will help familiarize students with the rights laid down in the Convention of the Rights of the Child. Discussion is likely to point up certain common features of rights abuses; i.e. that, in most cases, more than one right will be simultaneously under assault and that responsibility for rights denials/violations usually lies to varying degrees with more than one party. The final two columns focus on the all-important question of the kind of action that can and should be taken by children and adults individually and collectively, to protect the rights of young people.

'RIGHTING WRONGS' CASE STUDY TITLE:

Children's rights denied/ violated	Those responsible for denial/ violation of children's rights	Actions children have taken to protect their rights	Actions you think should be taken by children and adults to fully realize their rights

Nasreen, voice of outrage from a house under siege

John Pilger records the prolonged racial torment of an Asian family in east London, through the testimony of a teenage girl

Last week Nasreen phoned me to say: 'We have a new neighbour who is being nice to us. We are taking down the barricades and we are hoping for the best; but we are frightened.' I have known Nasreen and her family for four years and this is the first good news. Almost every night since they have stayed together in their one large room, overlooking their street in the East End of London. They seldom go out after seven o'clock at night, neither do they go downstairs after dark.

Only their dog, a worrying beast called Soldier, is downstairs, in the front room that was to be the father's tailor's shop and which they barricaded four years ago on the urging of the police, who said, in effect, they could do nothing about the attacks.

When I was there the other night, Nasreen's mother was sitting beside the window as she has done for four years, rarely moving from this watching position. Her bed has been moved there, and when she talks her eyes remain fixed on the street below. Beside her is a plastic box filled with antidepressants and sleeping tablets.

'At first they'd go in circles', said Nasreen, who is 19. 'They'd go round and round. Or maybe they'd just sit and do nothing at all. Or maybe, they'd just smash the door and throw rocks . . .'

'And shit', said her father, trying to smile. 'And shit', said Nasreen, '. . . through the letter-box, all over the hallway.'

Britain in the 1980s is a society in which large groups of citizens are virtually invisible. Extraordinary and often terrible events can happen in people's lives and there is little or no news about them; and there is official indifference. Racist attacks on Asian people – relentless and unchecked – are part of this pattern of silence.

Of course there will be an occasional piece in the papers or on television; more likely it will be in the ethnic press. Home Office statistics six years ago revealed that Asians were 50 times more likely to be attacked than whites. That figure is thought to be much higher today.

In spite of their public statements, the police are loathe to recognise racism as a motive for attack or harassment.

So widespread are racist attacks that on the Barking road, a major artery of the capital, Asian shopkeepers are terrorised almost casually by those who appear to be members of the same gang. Last November, an Asian man and his son were subjected to an horrific attack in daylight in Barking Road.

The father was slashed in the face with a knife, his nose was broken and he has spinal injuries. The son suffered head injuries and a broken hand as he tried to protect his father. What was unusual about this was not the nature of the attack, but that the police arrested four of the gang, several of whom were found 'celebrating' in a nearby pub, with blood on their clothes.

Two weeks ago, not far away, a young black man, Trevor Ferguson, went to confront a gang of whites outside a house where his friends were having a party. The gang was chanting: 'Kill the niggers!' and reportedly hurled teargas through the letterbox. Trevor was beaten so badly with bottles he was left with one eye hanging out and has now lost the eye. The police told the family they did not consider the attack racist. No one has been arrested.

Nasreen's family has known all kinds of attacks. The recent calm, and the interest of the police, are undoubtedly due to her efforts. For almost all her teenage 22 years, she has been the protector and voice of her parents who came here from Pakistan 22 years ago. She phones me often, several times a week. In the beginning she would say, in her Cockney accent: 'They're at the door now. Hear 'em? I've called the police and we're waiting. That's all. Bye.'

She would phone back to say they were all right: she was merely making contact with the world outside her barricades. She reminded me of Anne Frank, the Jewish girl who hid from the Nazis in the attic of her Amsterdam home. She is Anne Frank with a telephone.

The diaries Nasreen has kept are surely material for future historians who wish to look beneath the surface of Britain in the 1980s. The first entry was during the week they moved into their house. A gang of 40 attacked on 25th January 1983. The gang threw stones, smashing the shop windows and gave Nazi salutes. They shouted: 'Fucking Pakis out!' They were able to do this, undisturbed, for six straight hours. Nasreen wrote in her diary: 'When the trouble started we phoned the police, but they never came. Then again we phoned the police, but they never came. Then my father went to the police station to get the police . . . . we had a witness. The police said they didn't need a witness.'

The entries in the diary for the weeks that followed, often written by candlelight in freezing darkness as the family huddled in an upstairs room, were repetitive and to the point: 'Trouble. Got no sleep. Had no telephone . . . three or four of them throw stones at our window.'

One night when she phoned me, Nasreen described her life as 'sort of like living under a table'.

At that time Newham police told me they had given the family 'special attention', but that it was impossible to mount a '24 hour guard'. They suggested the family move from the 'trap' of the cul-de-sac they live in. Two auctions have failed to sell the house. Alongside Nasreen's diary is a growing file of correspondence with the police, the Home Office, the local authority, local MPs and the Prime Minister to do something about a family that were being 'smashed about by skinheads'.

Mrs Thatcher replied that the Home Secretary was 'taking up the matter'. The matter was never taken up. So Nasreen wrote to Mrs Thatcher this letter:

> *Dear Mrs Thatcher*
>
> *I am sorry to say you don't understand our matter . . . . you don't care if we get beaten up, do you? My mother has asthma and she has to stay to 11 a.m. watching through the window because me and my brother and sister has to go to school. I can't stay at home to look after my mother because I got exams to worry about. We have no money to repair our house since the kids in the street have damaged it. We are asking for your help, not your money, Mrs Thatcher.*
>
> *Yours sincerely*
> *Nasreen*

An extraordinary reply came, not from Mrs Thatcher but from a Mr C.D. Inge at the Home Office. Mr Inge urged the family to keep reporting every attack to the police, 'even if the police are unable to take effective action'. He then apologised for 'not being able to give you a more helpful reply'.

Source: *The Independent, c.* 1987

'I ain't sitting beside her'

Shyrose Jaffer records her ordeal in Ontario schools

I can still vividly remember my first Home Economics class in Canada. It was my first week in Grade 7 and I remember walking in late because I was still trying to figure out how to find my way around the school. Most of the students were already seated, waiting for the class to begin, and I confidently chose the first seat available and sat down. I hadn't even sat down properly when the Chinese guy beside me got up so forcefully that he knocked down his chair with a loud crash behind him.

'I ain't sitting beside HER', he yelled scornfully with disgust written all over his face.

It took me a few seconds to register the fact that he actually meant me. That there was something about me, something that everyone was aware of judging from their faces, that was terrible enough to make someone want to avoid me.

I still can't understand why I did it, maybe it was some kind of pride, but I actually stood up, collected my books and walked over to another chair (one that was sufficiently far from the others) and sat down without a word. There was pin-drop silence in the room for a few seconds, and then, as if the incident had never occurred, class began.

Later, I walked home and I remember playing the scene again and again in my head. I was crying because I had been rejected but I honestly didn't know why that kid had done that to me. I was 13 years old and until that day it had never occurred to me that I was different. It wasn't that I had led a very sheltered life when my family had lived in the Middle East because I had gone to school with a mixture of children of all colours, from different countries of the world. It was simply the fact that I had never before noticed the 'difference' between people of other colours and me.

It may seem hard to believe but I was actually unaware of the notion of racism. No one had ever prepared me for this concept that some people in the world are considered, by some, to be 'better' than others. Until that point in my life I had thought of myself like any other 13-year-old in the world. My sixth day in Canada, in that symbolic event in class, was the day that I experienced a certain change in my self-concept. It simply meant, 'This is what it means to be me, I am different. I am undesirable'.

We lived in downtown Toronto at that time. And I still can't get over the fact that children of many races (oriental, caucasian and black) found me an object of ridicule. I dressed like them, my English was at times better than theirs (my accent wasn't that pronounced, even at that time) and yet they called me names and rejected me. It just served to bring home the fact that everyone thought I was distasteful. I cried each and every single day for my first three months in Canada.

One day I was sitting in English class and 'Rick' kept calling me names across a few desks. Suddenly, I could take it no longer. I began to write in my English book. I wrote of all the things that people were calling me, how much it hurt, how much I hated Rick. Then I ripped off the page, walked over to the black supply teacher we had that day, handed it to her and went back to my seat. I just felt so good to get it out of my system and I wasn't a bit remorseful when she called me over and told me that the principal was waiting to see me in his office downstairs.

I can't remember his face but I do remember that he put his arms around my shoulder after he finished reading my letter. He asked me to fill in one of the blanks that I had left in one of the sentences but I remember that I didn't even know what that swear word meant at the time. We spoke for a while and he was kind but none of his words had any impact. All that I remember is the comfort I felt in having his arm around my shoulder. Next day, Rick wasn't in class. He had been suspended for a week and when he came back, he never said a word to me again. My parents were never notified and I don't think I ever told them about it.

Let Friends Cheat
Just when I started making friends (I let them cheat off my paper on tests to get them to like me), my family decided to move to Unionville, which is right in the centre of Markham. My whole public school was full of white children whose parents made over $35,000 a year. By the end of Grade 8 I had encountered another 'Rick' (three of them actually) and I did the same thing again: I spoke to my teacher who gave them and the class a big lecture and made the offenders speak with me privately and apologise to me.

When I started high school I was full of renewed hope and enthusiasm. I had won the coveted 'Actress of the Year' award in public school and had become quite popular. Little did I know that my troubles were just starting. I was the only 'brown person' (there was one black guy) among 2,500 high school students but that didn't really bother me until one day in Grade 9.

I had almost reached my locker when I saw something written on it (with marker) in huge black letters.

'Go home, Paki' it read, 'Back to India where you came from.'

I was trembling with rage and tears and I found myself unable to go near the locker. It would be so embarrassing if anyone realised that those words were meant for me. I wasn't even from Pakistan. Besides, Pakistanis aren't from India anyway. All sorts of thoughts were flashing through my mind – I was trying to console myself but it wasn't working.

Almost every day, throughout Grade 9, I found myself at the principal's office complaining about various sayings that kept appearing on my locker door and they would send a janitor down to wipe it off. Then it appeared as if someone was trying to break into my locker. I would find my combination lock malfunctioning or half-broken. I must have gone through at least 10 locks that year. Then they started covering the locks with masking tape or taping all the edges of the locker with shaving cream and once I reached out unsuspectingly to touch my lock and found it covered with spit.

I started getting nightmares about finding my locker full of snakes and spiders; my nightmares almost came true when I found my locker without a lock one day. I didn't have the courage to open it myself because I was afraid of what I'd find in there. When my friend opened it for me she found nothing inside. All my books had been stolen and exams were in two weeks.

Made Me Stronger
I have grown up a lot since then. Today I can honestly say, with conviction, that my experience made me into a very strong and confident person instead of letting racism push me into a little shell. I used it to grow as a person. I have literally made myself ask questions in class or speak in front of a large audience. And instead of letting myself feel shame, I have developed a love and pride for my culture and religion and often try to dispel myths and educate people about it.

My 10 years in Canada have taught me that racism will always haunt and follow you around because there is a lot that needs to be done to educate some people, even at university. The trick is to fight it.

Source: *Toronto Star*, 3 November 1991.

ACTIVITY 16

Age of consent

Time needed   One hour 10 minutes.

Resources   Four **task cards**; 30 sets of **viewpoint sheets**.

Procedure   The class divides into groups of seven or eight. Each group is given one of the **task cards** and a set of **viewpoint sheets** (one set per member) and asked to prepare for an Age of Consent Committee hearing. The Committee has been asked by government to sound out informed opinion as to the advisability of reforming the age of consent laws and to make recommendations. Groups are given 30 minutes to prepare for the hearing.

The hearing is chaired by the Committee and takes the form of a submission by each group, followed by questions from Committee members and then questions from the floor. Following the three submissions, the hearing is opened for general debate. The Committee then retires, considers and, after 15 minutes, announces its provisional recommendations.

Potential   A lively and challenging way of introducing students to the arguments surrounding UK age of consent law. In the debriefing following the Committee's announcement, students should be asked to comment on the respective merits of the cases put by the three groups and the decision reached by the Committee. Would reform be helpful at this time or should we let sleeping dogs lie?

Students should also be encouraged to reflect upon the implications of various reform suggestions for our understanding of the meaning of childhood.

Source   Material for the viewpoint sheet is drawn from Ian Katz's article 'Not so sweet sixteen' and Janice Warman's piece 'Sarah's story: "I was unlucky"', *Guardian*, 11 January 1991.

TASK CARD: Group 1

In UK law the age of consent for sexual intercourse for females is 16. Under the Sexual Offences Act of 1956 it is illegal for a male to have sex with a female under the age of 16 whether she consents or not. The maximum penalty for a male who has sexual intercourse with a female between the ages of 13 and 16 is two years' imprisonment; intercourse with a female under 13 carries a maximum penalty of life imprisonment. There is no age of consent for males but a female undertaking sexual activity with a male under 16 can be charged with indecent assault. The age of consent for homosexual activity between males is 18. There is no legislation on lesbianism.

Your group favours the maintenance of the law as it stands. Your task is to use the evidence with which you are presented to prepare the most persuasive case you can think of in support of your position. Be ready to present your case to the Age of Consent Committee hearing.

TASK CARD: Group 2

In UK law the age of consent for sexual intercourse for females is 16. Under the Sexual Offences Act of 1956 it is illegal for a male to have sex with a female under the age of 16 whether she consents or not. The maximum penalty for a male who has sexual intercourse with a female between the ages of 13 and 16 is two years' imprisonment; intercourse with a female under 13 carries a maximum penalty of life imprisonment. There is no age of consent for males but a female undertaking sexual activity with a male under 16 can be charged with indecent assault. The age of consent for homosexual activity between males is 18. There is no legislation on lesbianism.

Your group favours reforming the law so that the age of consent for females is reduced. Your task is to use the evidence with which you are presented to prepare the most persuasive case you can think of in support of your position. You can make additional recommendations if you wish. Be ready to present your case to the Age of Consent Committee hearing.

TASK CARD: Group 3

In UK law the age of consent for sexual intercourse for females is 16. Under the Sexual Offences Act of 1956 it is illegal for a male to have sex with a female under the age of 16 whether she consents or not. The maximum penalty for a male who has sexual intercourse with a female between the ages of 13 and 16 is two years' imprisonment; intercourse with a female under 13 carries a maximum penalty of life imprisonment. There is no age of consent for males but a female undertaking sexual activity with a male under 16 can be charged with indecent assault. The age of consent for homosexual activity between males is 18. There is no legislation on lesbianism.

Your group favours reforming the law so that the age of consent for females is increased to 17 or 18. Your task is to use the evidence with which you are presented to prepare the most persuasive case you can think of in support of your position. You can make additional recommendations if you wish. Be ready to present your case to the Age of Consent Committee hearing.

TASK CARD: Group 4

In UK law the age of consent for sexual intercourse for females is 16. Under the Sexual Offences Act of 1956 it is illegal for a male to have sex with a female under the age of 16 whether she consents or not. The maximum penalty for a male who has sexual intercourse with a female between the ages of 13 and 16 is two years' imprisonment; intercourse with a female under 13 carries a maximum penalty of life imprisonment. There is no age of consent for males but a female undertaking sexual activity with a male under 16 can be charged with indecent assault. The age of consent for homosexual activity between males is 18. There is no legislation on lesbianism.

Your group is the independent enquiry team, the Age of Consent Committee, set up to recommend whether or not UK law needs reforming. Your task is to cast a keenly critical eye over the evidence with which you are presented and to develop searching questions to put to the three groups which will appear before you. One group will favour maintaining the law as it stands, one will argue for reducing the age of consent for females and one will recommend its increase. You will have 15 minutes together as a group at the end of the hearing before announcing your provisional recommendations. Try to base your judgement upon the qualities of the arguments presented rather than upon your own opinions.

VIEWPOINTS

I began sleeping with my boyfriend at 14. I was pregnant at 16. When I told my boyfriend, he walked out on me. I was pregnant again, and got married, at 17. After a miscarriage and the birth of a daughter my husband left me. At 19 I was divorced, with another child on the way. The age of consent didn't help me. None of my friends were worried about breaking the law. They just said 'Oh, we're going to do it, and if we get caught, we get caught'. I think they should keep the limit at 16 but strengthen the penalties to make people think twice; that combined with better sex education in schools and free contraception. I don't regret having the children, but I would like to have got a good job and some money behind me before having them.

Janice, age 20

In the Netherlands we've reduced the age of consent to 12 providing parents approve and there is not a complaint. I'm baffled by the reaction of popular British papers like the *Sun* ('the sexual madhouse that is Holland'). The sexual act is still, in principle, forbidden to both boys and girls between 12 and 16. What's new is that if there's no complaint, there will be no prosecution. We had to bring the law up to date with reality. Thousands of young teenagers were having sex anyway.

Dutch Member of Parliament

If you set the speed limit at 30 everyone drives at 40. Set it at 40 and everyone will simply speed up to 50. The same principle applies to the age of consent. Reformers may be happy about 14-year-olds having sex, but that will simply encourage 13- or 12-year-olds. If anything, the age of consent should be raised to 18 as it is in countries like Italy and Portugal. That would at least afford more protection to the 16-year-olds.

British Member of Parliament

Young teenagers know they are breaking the law when they have sex. As a result a lot of young people are put off looking for help from school counsellors and bodies like us which provide sex counselling. Decriminalization of teenage sex would be the best way of encouraging teenagers to come forward for advice and, thus, tackling the soaring problem of teenage pregnancies (more than 66 per thousand among 15- to 19-year-olds in 1988).

Spokesperson for a Family Planning Advisory Centre

It is a denial of basic rights that the age of consent for heterosexual sex is set at 16 whilst sex is outlawed for male homosexuals under the age of 18. In the field of sexual rights in the 1990s, the key question is not that of lowering the age of consent for heterosexual teenagers but rather one of equality in law for homosexuals. Their age of consent should be reduced to 16.

Spokesperson for a civil rights organization

In what sense can an impressionable and immature 12- or 13- or 14-year-old consent to anything? She may be physically advanced for her years but can anyone seriously claim that she can arrive at a mature assessment of her feelings and best interests and then make a decision accordingly? How would a court decide consent with one so immature? Anyway, to reduce the age of consent would leave young teenage girls unprotected against abuse and harassment by teenage boys. A lot of sexual offences are committed by young people. This is something which is going to be big news in the years to come.

University professor

A study published today and carried out in the south-west shows that almost half the girls questioned (in a sample of 400) claim to have had a sexual experience before 16. More than one in three boys made a similar claim. So it seems, on the face of it, that there is a case for reconsidering our laws on consent, or at least considering reconsidering. After all, can it make sense to cling to a law which makes up to half of teenage girls party to a criminal act?

Article in the *Daily Mercury*

There is one big reason why the age of consent should not be lowered – sexual abuse. Throughout the 1980s the dark side of adult–child relations in the United Kingdom was exposed for all to see. The age of consent laws were traditionally viewed as protecting young girls from the perils of pregnancy, disease, exploitation and prostitution. They are now seen as one of the best weapons we have against the abuse of girls by men.

Social worker

I'd accept that girls need protection against abuse and exploitation by older men but what rankles with me is the way in which the letter of the law prohibits sex between consenting young teenagers. Why can't the legal age for sex between teenagers be reduced whilst retaining a bar on sex involving an older man, thus protecting girls against abuse?

Guidance counsellor

ACTIVITY 17
Whose job is it anyway?

Time needed	40 minutes.
Resources	A set of job cards (see p. 66) cut up and placed in an envelope for each group of five students; chart paper, felt-tip pens and a glue stick for each group; copies of the five extracts on child labour (pp. 67–70) for each group; Blu-tack.
Procedure	*Stage 1* The chart paper is divided into quarters with the following headings:

Jobs children under 13 should be allowed to do	Jobs children 13–17 should be allowed to do
Jobs only adults should do	Jobs no one should have to do

Working in groups of five, students discuss each job card in turn and decide the most appropriate section in which to place the card. Where two categories are felt to be equally appropriate, cards can be placed over the dividing line. Once a decision is made, the card is stuck down and an agreed reason or explanation for this choice is written, in brief, underneath. In cases of major disagreement amongst the group, students can decide either to accept a majority verdict, or to put such cards aside. Completed charts are stuck on the wall so that students can circulate and compare their categorizations as a precursor to plenary discussion.

Stage 2
Copies of the five extracts on child labour are given to each group, each student having one extract to read, assimilate and then describe in their own words to the rest of the group. In the light of these children's experiences, the group review their categorization of the job cards and make any agreed changes. Plenary discussion follows.

Potential

This activity is designed to challenge students' assumptions about the complex issue of child labour. In Stage 1 they will almost certainly use their own cultural perspective as a yardstick by which to categorize the various jobs, though there may still be considerable disagreement within a group. Class discussion could focus on the moral and legal issues that were raised (the law surrounding child labour in the UK is summarized in Activity 18). Did students assume that all the jobs under consideration were paid? Should there be a pay differential between children and adults engaged in the same work? To what extent was the categorization based on the students' own experiences of work?

In Stage 2 the extracts on child labour will force students to look at the issue from other perspectives. They may be surprised – even shocked – at the way children are exploited in parts of Europe, as well as in the developing world. Discussion should now focus on what changes, if any, were made to the groups' original classifications. To what extent were legal and moral considerations tempered by the arguments of economic necessity? In order to protect the rights and welfare of children, should the law acknowledge many families' need of child labour and provide appropriate safeguards, or should existing laws (restricting child labour to certain jobs at certain ages) be more strictly enforced?

JOB CARDS

textile worker	car washer
street seller	pop star
cleaner	executioner
lorry driver	agricultural worker
shoe shiner	spy
coal miner	actor
fire fighter	shop assistant
soldier	tennis player
window cleaner	car mechanic
child minder	prostitute
police officer	gardener
judge	dancer
dish washer	surgeon
paper delivery person	teacher
sewage worker	bartender

Children and work in Naples

Even the briefest visit to Naples will reveal to the often surprised tourist the existence of child workers. As you sit in any café you will see a 9- or 10-year-old boy flit in and out of office buildings carrying his tray of cups of coffee, or hanging around during his work break, with a cigarette dangling from his mouth in expert fashion. A more adventurous visitor, exploring the narrow streets of the old quarters of the city, will see small boys covered in grease helping out at a car mechanic's workshop or bicycle shop. And there are the small groups of boys practising guerilla warfare tactics on tourists, as well as those windscreen cleaners who make their services necessary by taking the precaution of wiping a dirty cloth over your windscreen as soon as the traffic lights turn red.

Children's paid work is usually parallel to schooling. Where there is a family workshop or other business, the children will almost certainly be expected to spend many hours helping out after school. Where the mother only is involved in production in the home, there may be less pressure but it is usual for little girls to help their mothers. Not so little boys, who help only (and this very casually) when they are quite young. As they grow older the sexual division of labour establishes itself: the mother is doing a woman's job and women and girls around her should help her and learn her skills. But both boys and girls may be apprenticed out to a neighbour or kin to learn a trade. The burden of carrying out two activities – or more in the case of little girls who may help in the home and work for money and go to school – is a heavy one. Absenteeism from school is high in certain areas of Naples and there is a tendency for numbers to drop progressively from the first grade onwards.

Source: V. Goddard in *Anthropology Today* 1 (5), October 1985.
Reproduced by permission of the Royal Anthropological Institute of Great Britain and Ireland.

Gracinda (Portugal)

We first met Gracinda trudging along the same busy road where two years before she had been knocked down, fracturing her skull and legs. To make enough to live on the patch of land on which they were building a small, single-storey breeze-block house, Gracinda and her mother had to work. They took home work from a nearby shoe factory. It was a large bag of half-finished shoes to be sewn that Gracinda was carrying when we met her. This was a half-hour walk along a road of which she was understandably frightened, but Gracinda's mother had been ill, and Gracinda had had to shoulder the burden of the work assigned to both of them, which brought in 2000 escudos a week, just £8.00. She worked each day from after lunch till midnight; and rose again at 5.30 a.m. to prepare her father's breakfast.

This was Gracinda's twelfth birthday. She thought it was another day, but she was confused. When she had recovered from her injuries, she had returned to school but was put in a lower class to make up for the year she had lost. Compulsory schooling stops at the age of 13 in Portugal, and although it is illegal to work until 14, Gracinda felt she could do more to help at home. So, where other children played, she stayed at home sewing shoes, the rough rasp of needle and thread on the leather sounding an appropriately harsh note in her bare bedroom. In this poor little room, it was as if she was sewing up her own life.

Source: P. Lee-Wright, *Child Slaves*. London: Earthscan, 1990. Reproduced by permission of Earthscan Publications Ltd.

Child prostitution in France

According to the Paris-based 'S.O.S. Enfants' 8000 French children are involved in organized prostitution – 5000 boys and 3000 girls. Those involved in coping with this problem believe that societies which place such an over-riding value on money, and in which children see people selling themselves in so many different ways, are partly to blame for the rise in child prostitution.

At the time I agreed to lift up my skirt I had the impression I was doing something momentous. And then afterwards I told myself 'That's all there was to it'. And from then on, it was true – that's all it was. (Girl, age 13)

In front of a cinema, a guy approached me and offered me money. At first I didn't want to agree, and when I did agree I was scared, but I wanted a skateboard so I went along. And it wasn't terrible, on the contrary it was actually nice. My parents found out about it, and the worst bit was when I told them 'It was nice'. My Dad went mad with rage, and he kept telling me, 'Say that again, say that again'. That's what he couldn't take. (Boy, age 14)

When I used to bring money home – and you know how poor we are – my father used to accept it because he thought I got it by begging. When he knew [it was through prostitution] he said he wanted me to stop, but how could he stop me? (Girl, age 14)

There are moments when I feel disgusted with myself, and then I feel shame, shame throughout my body. (Girl, age 13)

Source: *New Internationalist* **76**, June 1979.

Fortune Garment Factory, Bangkok

The Fortune Garment Factory is managed and owned by Mr Bundit Lertnimitr and his father and mother. In common with virtually all factory owners in Bangkok, they are overseas Chinese, and have been selling to the UK for about a decade. Mr Bundit has a virtue which one does not always come by in the rag trade. He is honest. He has a couple of hundred machines on the first and second floors of a building deep in Bangkok's Chinatown. In the alleyways behind there are three narrow dwellings he uses as dormitories for the nearly 250 girls working there. There is no air conditioning, few fans and the open toilets are often blocked.

Mr Bundit describes conditions in his factory as 'not good', largely because the girls have to sleep feet to feet on the rough floor of his dormitories. They retire at 11 o'clock, near midnight, they have to stay taking a bath until maybe one o'clock, and they don't complain. Then they are up again to begin working at eight o'clock the next day, seven days a week! Sometimes, which means a lot of the time, the girls work through the night. For this, his younger girls, who are in their early teens, are paid less than one pound a day, which is half the official Thai minimum wage.

There is no real overtime pay and wages are held back to keep his charges from leaving. Last year these girls made, Mr Bundit says, some 12,000 three-piece woven acrylic women's suits and 3500 similar two-piece suits, as well as thousands of sweaters. He was paid £4.74 for both the three-piece and two-piece outfits, which is cheap. The same garments were sold throughout Britain at £19.99.

There is, Mr Bundit explains, an unwritten agreement among the Bangkok factory owners not to put wages up without consulting the others. Few firms offer contracts, most prefer to employ girls on the basis of trust. 'No contracts, no problems', Mr Bundit succinctly explained.

Factory owners shy away from employing girls who have lived in Bangkok for fear that they are much too streetwise and can fend for themselves. Poor, illiterate, uneducated farm girls from Thailand's impoverished north and north-east are the employees of choice. They work hard, ask few questions, and don't complain. In effect, buying in Bangkok enables British firms to circumvent over 150 years of British social legislation.

Source: E. Harriman, 'Modern slavery', *New Statesman*, 10 February 1984

An Uneasy Calm (Angola)

Gervasio was 11 years old when he joined the rebel UNITA army in 1987. He says that he was thrown directly into combat, quickly equipped with a uniform, boots and an AK-47 submachine gun. He took part in many battles.

'Both my brothers were killed in the war – they were shot', says Gervasio, who has not seen his mother since last year and has no idea where his father is. But the present is all that matters to him as he sits on a wobbly stool at the Vila Nova demobilization camp for former soldiers about 30 miles from Huambo in central Angola.

Gervasio refuses to say whether he has killed anyone during the war. His friend Joao is more willing to discuss the subject: 'I killed five people', he says. 'They were all soldiers. It was self-defence.'

Still, the two boys say they are glad the war is over, even if they have no clear idea of what peace is like. Born during war, this demobilization camp is their link to civilian life. The Lusaka Protocol, a peace agreement signed in November 1994 by the Angolan Government and UNITA, stipulates among other things that 60,000 UNITA soldiers were demobilized into the centres.

Getting an education is obviously a top priority for former child soldiers, but many of them have never seen the inside of a classroom, except perhaps to find refuge. Joao is an exception: 'I went to primary school', he says. 'And I can read a little.' He wants to learn how to write and do arithmetic. Gervasio has a longer way to go – he doesn't know how to read or write.

Educated or not, both boys want to become truck drivers. 'So we can travel around and deliver merchandise – and wear a uniform and cap.'

Source: Damien Personnaz/UNICEF Features Service, from *The United Kingdom Committee for UNICEF Annual Review 1995/1996*

ACTIVITY 18
Labouring children

Time needed   Two hours.

Resources   Up to six blank cards per student; a paper chart for each group; Blu-tack; a set of printed cards (see p. 75) per group; copies of **Article 32** of the Convention on the Rights of the Child (see p. 72) and of **Child labour and the law** (see p. 76) for each group; a supply of self-stick notes.

Procedure   Students form groups of six. Working individually and without discussion, they are asked to complete a card for each of up to six regular paid jobs they held between ages 10 and 16 (one job per card). Each job card should give as much of the following information as the student is prepared to share: their age when they began and stopped doing the job, details of the type of work they performed, details of the days they worked each week, of the number of hours worked each particular day and of the times between which they worked, details of work conditions, hourly rate of pay. Students should be encouraged to make cards out for casual jobs, e.g. baby sitting, if they have had less than six regular jobs. The cards are collected and shuffled. The group takes the cards, one by one, and discusses whether the employer in question exploited the student or treated her fairly. It should be emphasized that pressure should not be applied to any group member to supply information beyond what is on the card or even to own the card. The card is then placed in one of the four columns on the chart.

Very exploitative treatment	Exploitative treatment	Fair treatment	Very fair treatment

Students are then given a set of printed cards (see p. 75) which are taken from examples given in *The Hidden Army: Children at Work in the 1990s* (Low Pay Unit, 9 Upper Berkeley Street, London W1H 8BY, 1991). These are discussed and also placed in a chart column. Students may decide at this point to change some – or all – of the placings of their own cards.

72

Article 32

1. States Parties recognize the right of the child to be protected from economic exploitation and from performing any work that is likely to be hazardous or to interfere with the child's education, or to be harmful to the child's health or physical, mental, spiritual, moral or social development.

2. States Parties shall take legislative, administrative, social and educational measures to ensure the implementation of the present article. To this end, and having regard to the relevant provisions of other international instruments, States Parties shall in particular:

(a)   Provide for a minimum age or minimum ages for admission to employment;

(b)   Provide for appropriate regulation of the hours and conditions of employment;

(c)   Provide for appropriate penalties or other sanctions to ensure the effective enforcement of the present article.

Source: *Convention on the Rights of the Child* (November 1989)

Groups are then given a copy of **Article 32** of the Convention on the Rights of the Child and asked to review their decisions further, changing cards from one column to another if necessary, in the light of its contents. Following this, copies of the **Child labour and the law** handout are distributed and groups asked to decide whether the child employment situations described in their own and the printed cards constitute an actual or *prima facie* contravention of UK child labour legislation. The symbol L should be added to work situations falling within the law and I to those judged to be illegal. In the case of the latter, explanations of why the situation described is illegal should be attached to the card using self-stick notes. Finally, groups circulate to review each other's work. A class debriefing follows.

Potential

A powerful activity likely to raise a host of issues that will, in many cases, be directly impinging on the lives of the students themselves. As such, it needs to be handled with great tact and sensitivity by the teacher, who should at all points emphasize that it is being undertaken for awareness-raising rather than investigatory purposes.

In the debriefing, groups can first be asked to comment on where, in the second stage of the activity, they placed the dividing line between what was exploitative and what was fair treatment. What differences were there between group members, generally and over specific cards? What were considered fair pay, reasonable work conditions and suitable hours? When they received the printed cards, did perceptions in any way shift? Was it felt necessary to change the placings of the written cards? To what extent did reading Article 32 of the Convention lead groups to further review their decisions? In the light of the case studies in the written and printed cards, is Article 32 sufficiently strong and comprehensive? How could it be strengthened?

> 'Animals are much more popular than children in Britain.'
> *– Frank Field MP, on the state of UK*
> *child labour legislation*

At an appropriate moment in the debriefing, class attention can be turned to the questions raised by the **Child labour and the law** handout. Were students aware what present UK child labour legislation laid down? Had employers, teachers, or parents ever explained it to them? What disagreements were there in groups over whether the employment described in a particular written or printed card was legal or illegal? Should there be a minimum wage for those under 21? Does the law seem clear enough? Is it insufficiently strong or is it too limiting on child labour opportunities?

Extensions

1. The final section of the activity, as described under *Procedure*, can be strengthened if the teacher also circulates a summary of local bye-laws on child employment.

2. Students, working in groups and then as a class, draw up their own Charter for Child Employment.

3. Students conduct a questionnaire survey of local employers, of teachers and parents, to ascertain the extent to which relevant adults are familiar with UK child labour legislation.

4. Students invite the person responsible for monitoring observance of child labour legislation to speak to the class and answer questions. In a few local authorities this will be the Juvenile Employment Officer (whose sole responsibility is to ensure the law is obeyed); in most local authorities it will be the Education Welfare Officer (whose record in this area will depend on what priority she gives child employment amidst her other responsibilities).

5. Students watch films (see p. 90) on child labour in other parts of the world and discuss their contents in the light of Article 32 of the Convention.

I used to work in a shop. I worked there for eight months and the first couple of months I was on 50p an hour. Then it went up to 80p an hour. I was working four hours a day Monday to Friday and nine hours Saturday. I had Sunday off.
15-year-old boy

I work in a hairdressing salon for 89p an hour, for nine hours a week.
14-year-old girl

I earn £1.50 a week for twenty hours' work door to door selling.
16-year-old boy

I used to do a job for a firm that dealt with lorries. I used to take scrap parts from the lorry and put them in a scrap bin.
14-year-old boy

I've got a job as a cleaner in a hotel, and a cleaner in a paper factory, but I clean up in the offices . . . I work on weekdays, on the night times . . . But whilst I'm on holiday I work on weekdays on morning shift, which is four hours long.
15-year-old girl

I nearly always sleep out on a Saturday but I'm unable to on Fridays because I work. I work every Saturday for my dad on a market stall where I sell faulty clothes. The day starts at 6.30 and finishes at 4.30, so by the time I get home I'm tired – but this wouldn't stop me from going out.
15-year-old girl

I work at a shop. It is my uncle's shop; I get paid every week . . . Every day after school I go to work at 5.00 and come back at 7.30 every day. Sometimes I go to cash and carries to bring things which we need in the shop. It is far away.
11-year-old boy

I earn £25.00 a week for three hours cleaning.
13-year-old girl

When I am not at school I work at my uncle's garage. I leave at eight o'clock to go there, and come back at nine o'clock.
15-year-old boy

I have five jobs: delivering newspapers, helping with a milk round, working in a clothing shop, helping with furniture removals and working in a take-away restaurant. I earn 50p an hour for ten hours' work.
11-year-old boy

Child labour and the law

UK law regulating child employment is based on legislation passed mainly in the 1920s and 1930s.

No child shall be employed:

* under the age of 13

* during school hours on any school day

* before 7 o'clock in the morning or after 7 o'clock in the evening on any day

* for more than two hours on any school day or on a Sunday

* to lift, carry or move anything so heavy as to be likely to cause injury

These rules cover any child working for an enterprise carried out for profit, whether or not the child is paid. Hence jobs such as baby-sitting or running errands are not covered by law as the employer is non-profit-making. Working for a family business *is* covered by the law in that profit is involved.

Children under 16 cannot:

* be employed in mining, quarrying, manufacture and repair, building construction and demolition, the electricity industry or passenger transport *unless* the business is one in which only members of the same family are employed

* be employed to drive an agricultural tractor or machine, operate a circular saw, handle poisonous substances, use equipment without the proper safety precautions or clean machinery where there is the threat of injury

* be employed in street trading, including markets and newspaper selling (the legal age is 17 unless the employer is a parent in which case the age is 14)

* be employed during opening hours in a bar or licensed premises or in a licensed betting office (the legal age is 18)

Other points:

* the Home Office recommends (but does not insist) that children under 16 should not be employed serving petrol

* employers are required to register, and obtain work permits for, all children under 16 that they employ *after* the child has begun work

* local authorities have the power to introduce bye-laws strengthening and updating national child employment regulations and many have done so

* in 1973 Parliament passed the Employment of Children Act, the aim of which was to reduce the confusion in child employment legislation by raising UK standards to those laid down by the most vigilant local authorities under their bye-laws. The Act was never implemented. A simple procedure – an order – from the Secretary of State for Health would ensure its immediate implementation. At a stroke, uniformity in child legislation would be achieved across all local authorities and, importantly, employers would have to register their intention of employing a child (giving the authorities time to assess the suitability of the employment).

ACTIVITY 19

Children's rights at school

Time needed   To be judged by the teacher according to context.

Resources   30 copies of the **Summary of the Convention on the Rights of the Child** (pp. 6–7), 30 copies of **Articles 28 and 29** (p. 79–80), a chart (see below) for each five students, six felt-tip pens, additional sheets of chart paper, cards, Blu-tack.

CLASSROOM	SCHOOL

Procedure   Students are each given a copy of the **Convention on the Rights of the Child** summary sheets and are asked to form groups of five. Their attention is drawn to Articles 2, 12, 13, 14, 15, 16, 17, 19, 23, 30, 31 and 37 (which have a bearing upon the classroom and general school situation). They are asked to convert each right into detailed classroom-specific or school-specific rights statements. For instance, 'the right not to be subjected to cruel, inhuman or degrading punishment or treatment' (Article 37) might trigger discussion around forms of punishment used in class and in the school generally and whether any of these are tantamount to a violation of the Convention. Out of the discussion, one or more rights statements – guarding against such violations – might emerge. These are written down on the chart provided.

One Board of Education in the United States listed the following as 'degrading' punishments:

— sarcastic remarks
— forced apologies
— personal indignity
— meaningless tasks
— frequent detentions

Source: *World Studies Journal* **6** (2) (1986), p. 4

The class then comes together in 'moot' session to share and vote upon their statements. This is, perhaps, best done by the chairperson (teacher or chosen student) guiding the class through each of the selected extracts and asking groups to read out and explain the classroom and school rights to which, in their opinion, it gives rise. The contributions of each group are written on the board or overhead transparency, discussed and then voted upon. Suggestions receiving the vote of two-thirds of the students are written up on chart paper and adopted as part of a School Charter of Rights.

Articles 28 and 29, which are education-specific, are then shown to the class and suggestions elicited about other possible inclusions in the School Charter. Suggestions are listed and voted upon in the same way.

Each of the agreed rights is written on a separate piece of card and put in a pile. Working in the same groups, students pick a rights card and compile a list of responsibilities that they and others will have to exercise if the right in question is to be fully enjoyed. Groups continue to choose new cards until the pile is exhausted. The class re-convenes in 'moot' and proceeds to compile a School Charter of Responsibilities as groups report back and their suggestions are put to the vote.

Students again return to their groups, this time to discuss what reforms might be necessary in terms of school organization, decision-making processes, consultative, grievance and disciplinary procedures, student–teacher relationships and curriculum to transform the school into a more rights-respectful institution. Ideas are brought to a further 'moot' session, discussed and voted upon, and a Reform Charter drawn up.

As a final stage, the class can invite one or more members of the senior management team (plus any available departmental and pastoral head) to listen to a presentation around their Charter of Rights, Charter of Responsibilities and Reform Charter. The invited panel respond and discussion follows.

Potential

An effective way of giving students experience of applying general rights statements to specific contexts, in this case a context in which they are a principal stakeholder. The activity also encourages discussion and reflection around the *responsibilities* generated by rights claims. An important discussion point might be: are there qualitative differences in the responsibilities laid upon students and upon others (especially teachers) in the rights-respectful school? For the final stage of the activity to be the important and meaningful event it can be, it is crucial that the invited senior and middle managers approach the occasion in an open-minded, serious, non-authoritarian and unpatronizing way.

ARTICLE 28

1. States Parties recognize the right of the child to education, and with a view to achieving this right progressively and on the basis of equal opportunity, they shall, in particular:

   (a) Make primary education compulsory and available free to all;

   (b) Encourage the development of different forms of secondary education, including general and vocational education, make them available and accessible to every child, and take appropriate measures such as the introduction of free education and offering financial assistance in case of need;

   (c) Make higher education accessible to all on the basis of capacity by every appropriate means;

   (d) Make educational and vocational information and guidance available and accessible to all children;

   (e) Take measures to encourage regular attendance at schools and the reduction of drop-out rates.

2. States Parties shall take all appropriate measures to ensure that school discipline is administered in a manner consistent with the child's human dignity and in conformity with the present Convention.

Source: *Convention on the Rights of the Child* (November 1989)

ARTICLE 29

1. States Parties agree that the education of the child shall be directed to:

(a)   The development of the child's personality, talents and mental and physical abilities to their fullest potential;

(b)   The development of respect for human rights and fundamental freedoms and for the principles enshrined in the Charter of the United Nations;

(c)   The development of respect for the child's parents, his or her own cultural identity, language and values, for the national values of the country in which the child is living, the country from which he or she may originate, and for civilizations different from his or her own;

(d)   The preparation of the child for responsible life in a free society, in the spirit of understanding, peace, tolerance, equality of sexes, and friendship among all peoples, ethnic, national and religious groups and persons of indigenous origin;

(e)   The development of respect for the natural environment.

Source: *Convention on the Rights of the Child* (November 1989)

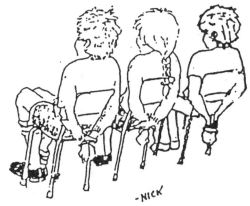

ACTIVITY 20
The scarf

Time needed   One hour.

Resources   A copy of **Political storm** article (see pp. 82–3) for each class member; two copies of the **list of interviewees** (see p. 84) for each group.

Procedure   Students are asked to read the article and to think themselves into the perspective of the three Muslim girls refused permission to wear their headscarves in class. The class then divides into six groups. Approaching the task from the girls' perspective, each group is asked to prepare for an interview with one of six people (see p. 84) who have some power or influence in the case. The teacher allots a different interviewee per group. In preparation for the interview they must determine answers to the following questions:

1. What can this person do to help us?

2. What has this person to gain/lose by supporting our cause?

3. What/who might this person have to fear if s/he supports us?

4. How can we make it easier for this person to support our cause?

Five minutes before the end of the preparation period, one member of each group detaches herself from the group, and works herself into the role of an interviewee other than the one considered by her group. She then joins another group in the role of the interviewee. The six interviews are role played. Class debriefing follows.

Potential   This activity is intended to help students better understand the complex situations in which people of power and influence often find themselves enmeshed whilst giving them training in advocacy skills. In the debriefing groups can be asked to explain the thinking behind their approach to the interview and to evaluate the success of their strategy in the role play situation. The class should be asked to identify effective advocacy strategies thrown up by their experience of the activity.

Extension   Groups re-read the article and identify rights listed in the **Convention on the Rights of the Child** (see pp. 6–7) which are being denied the three girls.

POLITICAL STORM BREAKS OVER MUSLIM SCARVES

Three Muslim girls determined to wear headscarves at school have caused an uproar in France. For over a week everybody, including the President's wife, have passionately discussed whether Muslim girls should be allowed to wear the *hijab* (headscarf) in state schools.

The Education Minister first stressed the importance of tolerance and obviously hoped that the schools which had forbidden the scarves would take the hint. They did not, so he was then forced to intervene. He made a statement that schools must first try to persuade the girls not to wear their scarves, but if they continued to persist they must not be deprived of their education as was happening at some schools.

'Schools should take children in, not exclude them', he said, pointing out that coming as they did from underprivileged backgrounds, the girls' future – and their integration – depended on their education.

The fuss began when the head of a secondary school in the Paris suburb of Creil told three girls that they could wear their scarves in the playground and in the corridors but must take them off in class. Two of the girls, scarves on heads, spent the week in the library and the third stayed at home. It was then suggested that the girls change schools or continue their education by correspondence.

The girls and their families have declined the offer and, instead, have engaged a lawyer. In a petition to the Education Minister the schools' 50 teachers asked him to intervene 'in order to restore peace quickly to the school'. The petition also stated that for some years various religious groups had been trying to assert themselves by ostentatiously flaunting exterior signs of their religions. The petition justified the head's *hijab* ban by pleading that such actions left them with no alternative but to insist that each group show 'a common respect for the norms of State education'. Pupils at the school are of 25 different nationalities.

Conflict on this issue is not restricted to Creil alone. In Montpelier, Marseilles and Avignon, Muslim girls are asserting their right to wear the *hijab* to school. In Montpelier, a 14-year-old Moroccan girl, Loubna Ryad, has been at home for the past month after being told at the beginning of term to take off the scarf she had already worn for two years in the same school. Her headteacher issued his ultimatum when five other pupils also arrived in scarves. Loubna's parents say they have not been able to find another school to take her – not even a private one.

Until now a minority of Muslim girls have been allowed to wear headscarves without any official objections, just as some Jews wear skull caps and Catholics crosses. And many state schools serve fish on Friday despite the fact that religion and religious instruction have no place in French schools.

The incident has revealed the difficulty the French are having with coming to terms with a growing Muslim population. Left-wing defenders of state schools resist any signs of religious infiltration, usually from the once dominant Catholicism. Their support for the schools forbidding the scarves has brought them into embarrassing agreement with the racist National Front.

Feminists and women's organizations argue that Muslim veils are closely associated with a view of women as second-class citizens, and that teenage girls are being manipulated by their families. Even the Muslim community is divided, with antiracist associations agreeing with the feminists.

Speaking in the National Assembly, the Education Minister warned that the girls would be expelled from school if they or their families attempted to persuade others to follow their example. He added that all pupils must respect their school's timetable and could not be exempted from gym or other classes on religious grounds.

Source: Abridged from an article by Mary Follain in the *Times Educational Supplement*, 3 November 1989, p. 18.

The interviewees

1. *The headteacher.* He runs a difficult school in an underprivileged area. The students come from 25 different national backgrounds. He is conscious that most of the teachers want decisive action because they are worried that the demands of the different religious groups will undermine order in the school. He is also keen to convince the governors of the school that he can be an efficient, firm leader.

2. *The Chair of the Board of Governors.* She is an ex-student of the school, a local politician (of the same party as the Education Minister) and a strong supporter of the state education system with its tradition of keeping religious observance and practice out of the schools. She owns a well-known local shop often frequented by members of the Muslim community. An election is looming and the majority she will be defending is small.

3. *The Imam at the local mosque.* He needs to defend the faith and the faithful but he is also concerned to build up cordial relations between the Muslim community and the wider society, not least because the Muslims need allies in the face of local right-wing hostility. His word, it is said, can significantly influence the Muslim electoral vote.

4. *Teacher at the school.* She has a good knowledge of Islam and is known to be sensitive to Muslim sensibilities. She is very approachable but is only new at the school and is, clearly, out of step with the thinking of most of her colleagues.

5. *The Minister of Education.* He does not wish to become embroiled in the details of what goes on in every school in the country and cannot afford to offend any religious group. He is keenly aware that the outcome of the Creil school case will send reverberations through many urban French schools.

6. *The editor of a national newspaper.* A firm believer in human rights, she is well known for supporting women's and ethnic minority causes through her editorials. She is keenly interested in human interest stories with a local flavour.

ACTIVITY 21
Organizing a school-based children's hearing

Time needed   Occasional periods of time over several weeks.

Resources   Postcards and sheets of paper.

Procedure   By means of an assembly or through an orchestrated series of
                         individual lessons, students are introduced to the Voice of the
                         Children International Campaign and the concept of children's
                         hearings (see pp. 8–11). They are reminded that under the
                         Convention on the Rights of the Child, Article 12, each child
                         has the right to be heard in all matters affecting him/her. It is
                         important for children to be heard, and it is just as important for
                         adults to be told in the children's own words what they are con-
                         cerned about: their hopes, fears, visions and demands for the
                         future.

                         Students are encouraged to take part in a children's hearing
                         process in the school itself, which will establish open channels
                         of communication between themselves and adult society and
                         representative decision makers. To begin the process they are
                         asked to do two things: firstly, to prepare a postcard (or letter,
                         poster, drawing or poem) expressing their ideas, concerns,
                         questions and demands about vital issues such as the state of the
                         environment, human rights, world peace, world development,
                         poverty and hunger; secondly, to elect a student committee to
                         organize the hearing (a male and female representative from
                         each year would produce a committee of reasonable size). The
                         committee would have the right to co-opt teachers to serve in an
                         advisory and supportive capacity.

                         The committee's initial task is to encourage students to send in
                         postcards, etc., and to collect and synthesize the views
                         expressed therein, the aim being to produce a concise, frank,
                         document – Children's Appeal – of no more than a few typed
                         pages, summarizing students' concerns. During this process,
                         the interest of the whole student body can be maintained by reg-
                         ularly producing a news-sheet and by committee members
                         occasionally reporting back to class or year groups.

                         The Children's Appeal should provide the basis for the school-
                         based children's hearing. The student committee sets a date and
                         invites parents, local politicians, local clergy, trade union and
                         media representatives and other decision/opinion makers to join
                         a panel (of six to eight members) to respond to children's views
                         and questions. The committee also invites applications from
                         students who would like to represent the views of the student
                         body and to actually address the panel (applicants should
                         explain which major world issues they are particularly con-
                         cerned about and should say why they would be a good choice
                         for the children's panel). The committee's task is to choose
                         about ten to twelve students for the lead role in the hearing

(those chosen should be representative of the student body in terms of age, gender and ethnicity and should have shown themselves, through their postcards and their overall contribution to school and local life, to be genuinely concerned about environment, development, human rights and peace issues). The choice of the student panel should be completed in sufficient time for chosen students to be able to brief themselves and carefully plan the content and sequencing of their questions/statements (using the Children's Appeal as their framework). They should also think about possible supplementary questions.

An invitation to the hearing, together with a copy of the Children's Appeal, should be sent to all students and their parents and the event should be widely publicized in the community. The media (local radio, press and television) should be invited. An exhibition of students' postcards, posters etc., should be displayed in the hall where the hearing is to take place.

A sympathetic, well-qualified mediator or ombudsperson should be invited to the hearing to chair the event firmly and to ensure that the questions/concerns raised by the students are directly addressed by the grown-ups without evasion (the person chosen should have time to talk to the students in advance). In addition, one or two experts on global issues should be asked along to clarify factual matters as and when called upon (they should be briefed about the questions to be put beforehand). It is also a good idea to include in the programme some student-initiated musical or dramatic entertainment relevant to the event.

At appropriate moments during the hearing the mediator should encourage contributions from children in the audience (but not from adults as their role, on this occasion, is to listen). It is a good idea to end the hearing by having one or more of the children read the Children's Appeal to the audience.

Encouragement should be given to the media to interview members of the students' committee and participating students; also to take photographs of the exhibition.

Potential

A demanding yet potentially hugely effective process offering students the opportunity to speak their minds to the adult world and to decision makers and opinion formers. Involvement in such a process, even if it leads to no immediate solid changes, can build in students a conviction that their collective actions can help create a better world. This feeling of empowerment is the most important objective in organizing a school-based children's hearing. Hence, the more the process is controlled by students the better. The event should be made known to the Secretariat of the Voice of the Children International Campaign (address opposite) and documentation (e.g. a copy of the Children's Appeal and newspaper cuttings) forwarded.

Students could then be sure that their views would also be noted in international fora.

It is recommended that the hearing should become an annual school event, providing students with the opportunity to put their view to local leaders and to hold them to account for promises made at previous hearings that remain unfulfilled.

Source   Voice of the Children International Campaign, c/o Kristin Eskeland, PO Box 8844 Youngstorget, 0028 Oslo, Norway.

The process itself is the real goal, to give children the opportunity to act, to speak their minds to the grown-up world. Whether their concerns are poverty, hunger, lack of housing or clean water, or worries about depletion of the ozone layer and the destruction of the rainforests, *the aim is to establish channels of communication between children and the adult society, between children and the decision makers*. Even if the grown-ups are unwilling or unable to take the children's views into account, the process, the involvement and activities of the children, have a value. No one can guarantee that politicians and other decision makers will take the children's viewpoints really seriously or that they are willing or able to take their opinions into account when final decisions are being made. But children's voices should be heard as well as the voices of other parts of society.

Children today are worried, often angry. They blame the adults for the problems, and rightly so. They get a lot of depressing information about the state of the world, they realize that their own future is at stake. A continued flow of information about environmental degradation, about poverty, hunger, war; coupled with a feeling that there is nothing they can do about it, no one is interested in their ideas, might lead to new generations of youngsters with no hope. They might turn into an aggressive group who would use any means to produce a change, or – much worse; a gang of frustrated, lethargic youngsters with no direction. As adults they are likely to have very little faith in their own ability to play an active role in the democratic process.

The Campaign Voice of the Children wants to prevent this from happening by giving active, knowledgeable kids a chance to speak their minds to the people in charge, by speaking TRUTH TO POWER.

Voice of the Children International Campaign

RESOURCES
1. Classroom resources

Alden, S. and Thynne, U. (1987) *Across the Divide*. A resource pack from Child Poverty Action Group (see p. 91) about poverty in the United Kingdom for the 14+ age group. Its activity-based approach will promote debate around the causes and effects of poverty and around the steps towards its relief.

Children First! A magazine published by UNICEF–UK (see p. 92) featuring articles on children's issues throughout the world as well as news on UNICEF's campaigning work in the UK. A useful source of information, including case studies and photographs.

Cruickshank, K. (ed.) (1982) *In a Strange Land I Live*. Sydney: Materials Production Project (Inner City Education Centre, 37 Cavendish Street, Stanmore, 2048, Australia). Stories and poems by, and interviews of, children from Asian countries who now live in Australia. The children, all attending Sydney high schools, tell of their experiences and of the problems they have had to confront at school and upon leaving school.

Exley, H., ed. (1985) *Cry for Our Beautiful World*. Watford, Herts: Exley Publications. An anthology of children's poetry and prose, collected from over 70 nations, with a common message: their future and the future of the planet are inextricably bound together. Beautifully illustrated by children, this book provides ample confirmation of the concern young people around the world have for the state of the planet.

Exley, R. and Exley, H. (eds) (1978) *Dear World*: '*How I'd put the world right*'. Watford, Herts: Exley Publications. A precursor, perhaps, to the idea of children's hearings (see Activity 21); the children (from over 50 nations) contributing to this book were all asked to tell adults how they would put the world right. The responses provide a delightful blend of idealism, humour, naivety and downright good sense. All are expressed with passionate concern for the world in which they are growing up.

Fyfe, A. (1982) *All Work and No Play: Child Labour Today*. London: TUC/UNICEF. Analyses the causes of child labour, examines means of combating it and explores children's rights. Designed for use with 16+ general and social studies courses.

New Internationalist. New Internationalist Publications, monthly. An excellent magazine on global issues, taking a theme each month. The articles are clearly written and presented; the double-page spread summarizing 'The Facts' in each issue is particularly suitable for the classroom. Past issues on children include: **76**, June 1979: *Children's Hopes for the Future*; **111**, May 1982: *Child Sponsorship*; **122**, April 1983: *Education*; **138**, August 1984: *Adolescence*; **143**, January 1985: *Choices for Youth*; **164**, October 1986: *Children's Rights*; **194**, April 1989: *Helping Children*; **240**, February 1993: *Girls and Girlhood*; **248**, October 1993: *Education*. Some past issues are still available.

Shah, I. (ed.) (1979) *World Tales*. New York: Harcourt Brace Jovanovich. A superb collection of 65 folk tales from all over the world, which demonstrates that some traditional tales are found in most cultures – the Algonquin Indian version of Cinderella presented is one of the 300 versions. Each tale is preceded by a short history and exquisitely illustrated by a leading contemporary artist. A treasure-trove of the world's folklore heritage.

Smith, L. (1988) *Dimensions of Childhood*. London: UNICEF–UK. A practical handbook for social education with the 16+ age range. Explores childhood in six dimensions: worldwide, multicultural, gender, hidden and social and economic.

Williams, R. (1987) *Children and World Development: A Resource Book for Teachers*. London: UNICEF–UK. Focuses on the situation of children and women in the developing world, showing what hunger, poverty, economic recession and other problems mean to those affected, with many statistics, diagrams and photographs.

2. Resources for the teacher

Bradshaw, J. (1991) *Child Poverty and Deprivation in the UK*. London: National Children's Bureau (8 Wakley Street, London EC1U 7QE). A UNICEF-commissioned study that estimates that the number of children living in poverty doubled in the 1980s. The study documents an increase in hopelessness, a deterioration in diet and increasing sickness amongst children. 'Black children, and their families', the author writes, 'are particularly disadvantaged on many fronts.'

Goodings, L. (ed.) (1987) *Bitter-sweet Dreams: Girls' and Young Women's Own Stories*. London: Virago. 46 young women speak out about their hopes and fears, their experience of school and university, jobs and unemployment, boys and girls, being different and racism, their expectations for the future.

Grant, J. P. (1994) *The State of the World's Children*. Oxford: Oxford University Press. Published annually on behalf of UNICEF, this is an indispensable source. Earlier editions are still very relevant.

Hoyles, M. (ed.) (1979) *Changing Childhood*. London: Writers & Readers. A collection of articles which challenge some dearly-held views and theories about children and childrearing. Includes a section on cross-cultural perspectives.

Hoyles, M. (1989) *The Politics of Childhood*. London: Journeyman. An ideological swipe at the alleged oppression of children by adults, principally in the UK. Argues provocatively for the politicization of children.

Lee-Wright, P. (1990) *Child Slaves*. London: Earthscan. Exposes the exploitation of child labour in the developing world (also Portugal, Turkey and the USA) and makes the important point that a substantial proportion of goods and commodities purchased in the West depend on such exploitation. Also explores sex tourism involving children in developing countries.

Moorhead, C. (ed.) (1989) *Betrayal: Child Exploitation in Today's World*. London: Barrie & Jenkins. Ten essays on international aspects of the rights of the child and the violation of those rights.

Pond, C., and Searle, A. (1991) *The Hidden Army: Children at Work in the 1990s*. London: Low Pay Unit (see p. 91). Based on a 1990 study of children in 13 Birmingham schools, it offers a shocking indictment of the ragged and ineffective nature of UK child employment legislation. Valuable reading before attempting Activities 17 and 18.

Postman, N. (1985) *The Disappearance of Childhood*. New York: Comet. An interesting thesis suggesting that the printing press created childhood by providing 'secret knowledge' only available to literate adults. Television, the argument continues, is causing childhood to 'disappear' by broadcasting information which is readily accessible and often more easily decoded by children than by adults.

Rosenbaum, M. and Newell, P. (1991) *Taking Children Seriously: A Proposal for a Children's Rights Commissioner*. London: Gulbenkian Foundation (98 Portland Place, WIN 4ET). Detailed proposals for the creation of a Children's Rights Commissioner, an independent statutory office to promote the rights and interests of children and young people.

Ross, J. and Bergum, V. (eds) (1990) *Through the Looking Glass: Children and Health Promotion*. Ottawa: Canadian Public Health Assocation. A collection of studies by experts in health care, anthropology and education on childhood, childrearing, child abuse and health promotion amongst children in different cultures.

Stanford, P. (ed.) (1988) *Hidden Hands: Child Workers around the World*. London: Collins. Provides profiles on children as well as poems from UK children.

Vittachi, A. (1989) *Stolen Childhood*. London: Polity Press/North South Productions/Channel Four. A comprehensive guide to children's rights – and denials of those rights – worldwide.

Woodhead, J. and Woodhead, M. (1990) *All Our Children: A Window on the World of Childhood*. Letchworth, Herts: Ringpress. Explores the experiences of childhood in over 15 different countries, the conclusion ringing from the pages being that there is no such thing as a 'normal' childhood.

3. Audio-visual materials

(Addresses of organizations are on pp. 91–2 if not given here.)

Chains of Tears, video, 52 minutes. Explores the plight of individual children in war-torn Angola, Mozambique and South Africa. Available on hire from Concord Film Council.

Child Slaves. Three films on exploited child labourers. Part 1, *The Slave Legacy*, explains child labour on present-day plantations; Part 2, *The Export Connection*, looks at child labour being used to maximize profits; Part 3, *The Moral Factor*, explores the cultural and economic factors pushing children into prostitution. Some disturbing sequences; hence, use judiciously. Each part, 25 minutes long, available on hire from Anti-Slavery International (free loan to ASI members).

Growing Up in the World Next Door, film/video, 59 minutes. A film about coming of age in developing countries. Bikas from Nepal, Michael from Kenya and Patsy from the Caribbean are seen at age 12 and again at age 18. All three were touched in some way by an international development project. Has the aid helped? Will it enable them to realize their goals and dreams? Available from the National Film Board of Canada, Box 6100, Station A, Montreal, Quebec, H3C 3HS, Canada.

Kids United, film/video, 27 minutes. Looks at the growing demands for rights by teenagers in residential care. Available on hire from Concord Film Council.

Refugee Children (1987), video, 40 minutes. Focuses on: Fatima, a 10-year-old girl from Chad living in a refugee camp in western Sudan; Antonio and Maria, who escaped from Guatemala to Mexico after their parents were killed; Nhue, a Vietnamese girl who lives with her mother and sister in a refugee centre in Hong Kong. Available on free loan from the Refugee Council.

Samroeng Case, video, 30 minutes. Study of a child bonded labourer in Thailand. English version of a Norwegian film. Available on hire from Anti-Slavery International (free loan to ASI members).

Stolen Childhood, video, 20 minutes. An introductory video on the rights of the child covering most of the major rights issues. Available for purchase from North South Productions, 1 Woburn Walk, London WC1H 0JJ.

Street Children, video, 20 minutes. Explores the growing problem of homeless and abandoned children living in cities. Children, such as Pinocio and Raul living on the streets of Bogotà, talk about what life is like for them. Available on purchase from UNICEF-UK, on hire from Concord Films Council.

The Best We Have to Give, video, 30 minutes. How are child survival programmes influenced by wider economic issues? This film looks at Ghana's attempts to provide for the basic needs of the child when burdened by massive international debt. Available from Asterisk Film & Video, 703–110 Spadina Avenue, Toronto, Ontario M5V 2K4, Canada. Tel. 001 416–868 1175.

What is UNICEF? 27 minutes. For children aged 12 and under, explains the work of UNICEF using children of Gospel Oak Primary School in London as a link with UNICEF's work in Angola, Bangladesh, Colombia and Nigeria. The video covers five specific subjects: clean water, nutritious food, health care, the rights of the child, how UNICEF began. Accompanying booklet with additional information and follow-up activities. Available on purchase from UNICEF-UK, on hire from Concord Films Council.

Who Cares? The Story of an Indian Girl, film/video, 21 minutes. The story of Rathna, a 19-year-old girl from a poor Indian village paralysed for a long time. She gains a place at a centre which helps severely physically disabled children to overcome their disadvantages. Available on hire from Concord Film Council.

Moving Pictures Bulletin **5**, April 1989, has a special supplement reviewing films on children. It is available from the TVE UK, 46 Charlotte Street, London W1P 1LX.

4. Useful addresses

Action for Children Campaign, P.O. Box 15, Northampton NN5 5QB, Tel. 01604–584264.
    Spearheads the United Kingdom and Ireland programme in support of the international campaign to 'End Child Prostitution in Asian Tourism' (ECPAT) and against child exploitation through sex tourism generally.

Amnesty International British Section, 99–119 Rosebery Avenue, London EC1R 4RE. Tel. 0171–814 6200.
    Has a Working Group for children that seeks to raise public awareness of the plight of child victims of human rights abuses. The Working Group publishes a quarterly newsletter. Schools can join the Group's campaign and write to political leaders around the world on behalf of specific children whose rights have been violated. Catalogue of audio-visual materials available.

Anti-Slavery International, The Stable Yard, Broomgrove Road, London SW9 9TL. Tel. 0171–924 9555.
    Exhibitions on child slavery and labour for borrowing; video cassettes and slide sets for hire, publications list available on request.

Children's Legal Centre, 20 Compton Terrace, London N1 2UN. Tel. 0171–359 6251.
    An organization concerned with law and policy affecting children and young people in England and Wales. It aims to promote the recognition of children as individuals participating fully in all the decisions affecting their lives. Briefing papers on topics such as access to school files and records.

Child Poverty Action Group, 1–5 Bath Street, London EC1V 9PY. Tel. 0171–235 3406.
    CPAG researches into poverty in the UK and campaigns for improvements in both benefits and other policies to bring about its eradication. Pack for schools (see *Classroom Resources*, p. 88).

Concord Video and Film Council, 201 Felixstowe Road, Ipswich, Suffolk IP3 9BJ. Tel. 01473–715754/726012.
    Films available for hire on child-related issues.

Defence for Children International, P.O. Box 88, CH-1211 Geneva 20, Switzerland. Tel. 0041–22–7340558.
    International non-governmental organization, the sole purpose of which is the promotion and protection of children's rights. Publishes the quarterly *International Children's Rights Monitor*. Publications list available. The United Kingdom section, DCI–UK, is based at Memorial School, Mount Street, Taunton, Somerset TA1 3QB. Tel. 01823–256936.

Equal Opportunities Commission, Overseas House, Quay Street, Manchester M3 3HN. Tel. 0161–833 9244.
    Offers advice/information on gender equality in schools and guidelines on sexual harassment.

Low Pay Unit, 9 Upper Berkeley Street, London W1H 8BY. Tel. 0171–262 7278.
    Undertakes research on, *inter alia*, child employment in the UK.

National Society for the Prevention of Cruelty to Children, 42 Curtain Road, London EC2A 3NH. Tel. 0171–825 2500.
    Research reports on child abuse trends in the UK and (free) parental guides on understanding and listening to children and on child abuse.

Refugee Council, 3–9 Bondway House, Vauxhall, London SW8 1ST. Tel. 0171–582 6922.
    Print and audio-visual materials on refugees.

Save the Children, Mary Datchelor House, 17 Grove Lane, Camberwell, London SE5 8RD. Tel. 0171–703 5400.
    Produces activity packs for the classroom (free catalogue available) and *Linx*, a quarterly magazine on children and development. A few videos for hire.

Scottish Refugee Council, 317 Cowgate, Edinburgh. Tel. 0131–553 5963.
    Provides speakers within the local area on refugee-related topics.

United Nations High Commission for Refugees, P.O. Box 2500, CH-1211 Geneva 2 Depot, Switzerland. Tel. 0041–22–7398111.
    Publishes the monthly magazine *Refugees*. Number 54 (June 1988) offers a dossier

on refugee children. Also publishes a selected and annotated bibliography on refugee children in co-operation with Save the Children Alliance, P. Boks 505, Sentrum 0105 Oslo 1, Norway.

UNICEF-UK, 55 Lincoln's Inn Fields, London WC2A 3NB. Tel. 0171–405 5592.
Offers print-form and audio-visual materials for schools (free catalogue available) and publishes *Children First!* three times a year, a lively magazine reporting on children's issues worldwide. The *Convention on the Rights of the Child Information Kit* is available for a small sum.

Voice of the Children International Campaign, c/o Kristin Eskeland, P.O. Box 8844 Youngstorget, 0028 Oslo, Norway. Tel. 0047–2–331590.
Orchestrates and monitors children's hearings (see Activity 21) at school, local, provincial and national levels, often through national committees.

INDEX